A History of the Shutting of the Gates Celebrations 1775–1985

A History of the Shutting of the Gates Celebrations 1775–1985

By

Albert Jackson

Copyright © 2022 by Albert Jackson

All rights reserved. No part of this book may be reproduced or used in any manner without written permission of the copyright owner except for the use of quotations in a book review.

For more information, address: albertjackson88@btinternet.com

FIRST EDITION

ISBNs:
Paperback: 978-1-80227-785-2
eBook: 978-1-80227-786-9

Dedicated to the memory of the three Roberts

Contents

Introduction 1

Chapter 1   The Two Big Days 5

Chapter 2   The Lundy Builders 19

Chapter 3   We'll Fight and Not Surrender! 51

Chapter 4   Their Cannons did Roar! 127

Chapter 5   More Lundy's 141

Chapter 6   Lesser Known Facts about the Eighteenth December
Celebrations 155

    Walker's Sashes 155
    The Shutting of The Gates Ceremonial Tradition 156
    Lundy's Boots 158
    The Traditional Burning of Chimneys 160
    Change of Date for The Burning of Lundy 161
    Payment for the Building of the Lundy Effigy 162
    Bands – The Browning Memorial Wreath 164
    The Crimson Ball 166
    Catholic Participation in The Shutting of
    The Gates Celebration 172

 The Flags, Banner and Lights on Walker's Pillar............................ 174
 Lundy Songs... 175
 List of people who had the privilege of setting fire
 to the effigy of Colonel Robert Lundy 186
 A List of those who placed a wreath on the Apprentice
 Boys of Derry Mound in the churchyard of St Columb's
 Cathedral, on Lundy's Day. 191

Bibliography 194
 Other Publications... 195
 Newspapers 195
 Unpublished Sources... 196
 Oil Paintings.. 196

Appendix 1 198

Introduction

To the visitor engaged in Christmas shopping, the spectacle of marching bands, Apprentice Boys and a huge straw effigy of Colonel Robert Lundy hanging from a scaffold erected in Bishop Street, would be bewildering. "What's it all about?" is the usual comment made by strangers, as they witness the annual Shutting of the Gates Celebration. Baffling as it is to the stranger, some members of the Apprentice Boys of Derry Association fare no better. Many stories have been told about Lundy, one being that he was so hungry during the Siege that he willingly handed over the keys of Derry's gates to King James for a bap. Another, that Lundy was really a supporter of King James and a traitor to the cause of King William III in Ireland. These are stories that are often related as truthful facts. Confusion and speculation go hand in hand as the myths increase about the real character of Lundy and why he should be burned in similar style to those who follow the Guy Fawkes tradition. This book is written to help answer some of the various questions asked about the Shutting of the Gates Celebration and its origins. Presenting some new information and setting it within a historical context will provide the reader with some understanding of the many components that make up an 18th December Celebration.

Oral and written historical records are important resources for interpreting and understanding cultural identity. They help to explain why something is celebrated in a particular way. The information that they present helps shed understanding on why the Celebration is important to some people's cultural identity. It doesn't mean that the event is celebrated by the community as a whole. It does show that differences are respected by the majority of people from different backgrounds, as the traditions have been allowed to continue through generations.

Maybe a better understanding of why the Apprentice Boys of Derry celebrate the two key Siege events – the Shutting of the Gates in December and the Relief of Derry in August – is best understood in terms of historical remembrance or collective memory, where history is remembered by a cultural tradition as an act of commemoration and not an act of triumphalism. The City of Londonderry has in the past been portrayed as the flagship of cultural inclusiveness, where two strong cultures that were once tinged with sectarian identity have overcome their difficulties and developed a mutual respect and understanding of each other.

The Apprentice Boys of Derry Association remains committed to respecting cultural diversity. The Apprentice Boys tried to keep the Association free from political sectarianism during the Troubles. The Troubles did have an impact on some of the Apprentice Boys General Committee decision-making processes, especially during the banning of all parades in the City in the late 1960s and early 1970s. It is at this point in history that the term *'loyalist'*[1] comes more to the forefront as a word used to describe someone's cultural identity. Loyalism demanded strong leadership, resolve and determination, to ensure that the Siege

---

1 The term *'Loyalist'* in this context must not be confused with the loyalist sectarian groups that would emerge during the height of the troubles in Northern Ireland. In the context of this study, it means those who want to remain true to their cultural identity and have the freedom to respectfully display it.

INTRODUCTION

Celebrations did not become an anathema. Different opinions in relation to imposed Bans nearly caused a split in the Association between its Branch members and the senior leadership of the General Committee. The latter part of the chapter 'We'll Fight and Not Surrender' will help to illustrate the real tensions that existed between factions of the Association membership and loyalists (in the wider sense of the word) who struggled to keep the Shutting of the Gates Celebration alive (better known as the 18th Celebrations).

The history of the Apprentice Boys of Derry Association and especially various Club origins has been well documented by C D Milligan. However, with careful scrutiny, some gaps in the historical narratives of the Association do appear. More could be said about the origins of the Shutting of the Gates Celebrations and why an effigy of Lundy burned in the City in 1788. Difficulties associated with the Apprentice Boys of Derry Organisation from the middle of the 19th century onwards could be discussed in more depth. And finally, more information about what the early Lundy effigies looked like could be discussed. This book sets out to present further information and explanation of the Shutting of the Gates Celebrations down through the centuries, by looking at every aspect of the Celebration.

The aim of the book is to present a simple history of the cultural tradition and heritage I grew up with. I am indebted to the Central Library for the use of their local newspaper archives and to the various authors whose publications I have read and quoted. I would like to thank my family for their help, support and encouragement over many years as I have collected resources and photographs in preparation for the publication of this book.

CHAPTER 1
THE TWO BIG DAYS

The Apprentice Boys of Derry Association was formed to perpetuate the memory of the Siege of Londonderry 1688-89. To achieve this, the Apprentice Boys of Derry Association in its infancy sought to remember the Siege by celebrating two annual events each year, better known as 'The Two Big Days', namely the Relief of Derry (12th August) and the Shutting of the Gates (18th December). It was a bold, yet significant move by some of the actual defenders and their ancestors, to ensure that the events of the Siege and the gallantry of the City defenders should never be forgotten in the annals of Irish history.

One of the prime movers among the defenders of the Siege was Colonel John Mitchelburne. Colonel John Mitchelburne had distinguished himself during the Siege and shared the Governorship of the City along with Reverend George Walker, after the death of Governor Henry Baker on 30th June 1689.

Colonel John Mitchelburne recognised the importance of celebrating the raising of the Siege, and so it was through his leadership and organisational skills that measures were put in place to ensure that the Siege of Londonderry would be remembered annually in the City. The

Colonel gathered fellow defenders around him who had survived the Siege and they met in St Columb's Cathedral on 1st August 1718. Prayers were offered by William Nicolson who was Bishop of Derry (1718-1729) and who had just arrived in the City a few weeks earlier. Bishop Nicolson was the first to record this event in his diary, *"Col Mitchelburne's Bloody Flag being hoisted ye first time on ye Steeple."* Great guns were discharged and volleys fired and that the evening concluded with a *"splendid treat in ye Tolset. Fireworks and illuminations."*[2] Two years later, Bishop Nicolson records again that on 1st August 1720, Mr Ward preached at the Relief of Derry Service in the Cathedral and that Colonel Mitchelburne, Dr Squire and Mr Blackhall dined with him in the Bishop's Palace. Later that night bonfires were lit in the City. Bishop Nicolson's diary records the earliest date of bonfires being lit in the City to commemorate the Relief of Derry Celebrations, a tradition that continues up to this present day.

The Siege commemorations occurred long before the official recorded date of 1718. C D Milligan makes an interesting note in his book *Colonel Mitchelburne, Defender of Londonderry and The Mitchelburne Club of Apprentice Boys of Derry: Centenary of the Revival of the Club, 1854-1954,* that the first Relief of Derry Service and its Celebrations took place during the Bishopric of William King. Bishop King arrived in the City on January 1691 and remained in office until 1702, when he was appointed Archbishop of Dublin. It was during Bishop King's period in office that the two French flags captured at Windmill Hill during the early hours of the 6th May 1689, were placed in the Cathedral by Colonel Mitchelburne while he was still Governor of the City (1689-92). Milligan suggests that the placing of these two flags in the Cathedral by Colonel Mitchelburne must

---

2 Hempton, John. *The Siege and History of Londonderry* (1861) p 411

have happened sometime between 1691-92. This is in itself is significant in that Bishop William King was an ardent supporter and defender of both the Church and the Protestant cause in Ireland during the reign of King James II. The Bishop deemed it right and proper that the two captured colours should be received by himself and placed at either side of the east window for perpetuity. The strategic placing of the two captured flags at either side of the Cathedral's east window was also significant. They would prove to be a timeless reminder to all who would visit the Cathedral of the Great Siege of 1688-89, and of the spirited resolve of its citizens; people who, by God's grace, were delivered them via the breaking of the boom on the evening of Sunday 29th July 1689. The Siege historian, John Hempton, also affirms C D Milligan's position, that it was during the Bishopric of William King that the Mitchelburne's captured colours were placed in the Cathedral and that *"This is the earliest record of a commemoration of the siege we have yet discovered."*[3]

Captain Thomas Ash, a defender of Derry, records an earlier account in his diary that the citizens of Londonderry celebrated the raising of the Siege on 8th August 1689. Ash writes:

> *"A sermon was preached before Major-General Kirk by Mr (Rev) John Knox setting forth the nature of the siege and the great deliverance which from Almighty God, we have obtained. In the evening all the regiments in the garrison were placed around the walls; they fired thrice, and thrice the great guns were discharged."*[4]

---

3 Hempton, John. *The Siege and History of Londonderry* (1861) p 403
4 Hempton, John. *The Siege and History Of Londonderry* (1861) p 419

A HISTORY OF THE SHUTTING OF THE GATES CELEBRATIONS 1775–1985

What is clear from the earliest documentation about the Relief of Derry Celebrations is that St Columb's Cathedral played a pivotal role in the day's Celebration. Siege descendants would gather to worship God followed by some sort of military display, the discharge of canon and a glass or two in the local ale houses in the City. Much more could be said about the Relief of Derry Celebrations, but recent historians have explored and documented their findings and the nature of this chapter is not to cover old ground, but rather to explore the development of the 18th December Shutting of the Gates Celebrations.

The history and development of Derry's second 'Big Day,' namely, the Shutting of the Gates on December 7th old style, does not emerge from the annals of history until the late 18th century. There are only two early recorded references to what was once a much lower key event compared to that of the Relief of Derry Celebrations in the month of August. The first reference appears on 7th November 1775 in the local newspaper. This was an appeal by Alderman Alexander, who was so impressed by the Relief of Derry Celebrations, that he sought to do something similar, only this time focusing on the heroic role that the thirteen Apprentices played in shutting the City gates in the face of Lord Antrim's forces. Alderman Alexander's appeal was directed to:

> "*The Mayor, Aldermen, Sheriffs, Burgesses and Freemen of the City of Londonderry to dine with him in the Town Hall, on Thursday 7th Dec, 'the anniversary of the day on which their gallant ancestors bolted their Gates bravely defending the City against invaders of their country.'* "[5]

---

5   Milligan, C D *Browning Memorials* (1952) p 9

Alderman Alexander further flatters himself by stating that descendants of those heroes will appear to celebrate the day and to drink a toast to their representatives at dinner at three o'clock in the afternoon. There is no mention of a Divine Service in the Cathedral or of any discharge of cannon to celebrate the occasion. Alderman Alexander in offering this invitation to the Mayor (Charles McManus) and fellow City dignitaries carried with it an alternative motive, namely the election of his brother Mr James Alexander to the House of Commons, who was later raised to the dignitary of Lord Caledon. Whatever one may think of Alderman Alexander, he did instigate the first December Celebrations ever to be held in the City to commemorate the Shutting of the Gates, via a dinner in the Town Hall!

The second reference to the Shutting the Gates Celebration appears in the *Londonderry Journal and Donegal and Tyrone Advertiser* dated 14th November 1775. This event was organised by the Leather Aprons and was reactionary. This reference highlights two important facts:

- The Leather Aprons, according to C D Milligan, was another earlier name used to refer to the Apprentice Boys of Derry Association (i.e. the young apprentices who shut the gates were all apprentices in their respective trade hence 'leather aprons', which they would have all worn). By now they were well organised, determined in purpose and loyal to the memory of the Brave Thirteen. The re-emerging of the Independent Mitchelburne Club, formed by Mr Thomas Anderson in 1775, seems to have been a combination of the old 1 & 2 Clubs (formed in 1772 and so called in reference to the number of guns/cannons they possessed), the Sons of Liberty Club and Phoenix Club (formed in 1773). Combining members

Lundy effigy tied to the Plinth of Walker's pillar in 1924.

Rare image of the upper half of Lundy standing up in the old lodge room in the Apprentice Boys Memorial Hall in the middle/late 20's.

A larger and more colourful Lundy hanging on Walker's Pillar during the late 20's early 30's.

A larger and much more elaborate uniformed Lundy in the 1960's.

Last Lundy made by the Jackson family in 1985.
Standing over 19 feet tall and weighing over a ton in weight.

from these redundant clubs strengthened the position of the new Independent Mitchelburne Club, which would play a vital role in the ensuing two main Siege Celebrations.

- Secondly, a class distinction emerges quite clearly from the two advertisements for the December Celebrations. Alderman Alexander's segregation of the lower-class descendants of Siege heroes from his Celebrations is quite clear when his guest list is examined. The Leather Apron's reacted against Alexander's segregated invitation by establishing their own format of Celebration, which was not entirely dissimilar to Alexander's, except for location - Mr Bradley's Hotel in Gracious Street (now Ferryquay Street). The foundation upon which this class distinction emerges can be clearly identified in The Act of 1704 to 1780, which banned Presbyterians from the City's Corporation. The tensions that already existed between non-Conformists (mainly Presbyterians) and Conformists (Church of Ireland) within the City resulted in a strong sense of political and religious segregation, betrayal and undermining of social status, of those whose ancestors had equally fought and suffered during the Siege of 1688-89. Post 1780, inter-Protestant tensions within the City had eased but not ceased.

By 1776, the True Blue Society, the Mitchelburne Company of Volunteers (1778), the Londonderry Independent Company of Volunteers (1778), the Apprentice Boys Company of Volunteers (1778), the Londonderry Fusiliers (1778), the Blue Volunteers (1780), the Corporation of the Guild Trades of the City of Gates against the forces of the abdicated King James (1780), the Derry Battalion of Militia (1780), The Londonderry

Regiment (1781) and the first company of the Independent Volunteers 1789), all played a major part in the Shutting of the Gates Celebration. They paraded to the Cathedral for a Divine Service, and an enactment of the shutting of the old City gates, firing the usual three volleys of shots in the Diamond, followed by the usual evening entertainment of food, drink and song in the Town Hall.

By the centenary year of 1788 a harmonisation of both social classes emerges with the sole purpose of celebrating the Shutting of the Gates. The Corporation and Clergy alike unite to celebrate this historic event with great pomp and circumstance. Local historical sources reveal a number of events, and several exist to this present day. The Divine Service in St Columb's Cathedral, the firing of cannon, the parading of various clubs, and the burning of an effigy of Colonel Robert Lundy in the Market place in the Diamond. This was the first recorded account of an effigy of Colonel Robert Lundy being burned in the City on 18th December. The December Celebrations in 1788 also provided the first documented account of Roman Catholic clergy being included in the Celebrations. The Reverend Lynch, who was the Roman Catholic clergyman in the City at this time, processed along with other City clergy to a Divine Service in St Columb's Cathedral to commemorate the Shutting of the Gates. By 1789, relationships between Protestant and Roman Catholics in the City were good, so much so that at the 1789 December Celebrations, the Roman Catholic Bishop Dr MacDevitt and several of his clergy took part in the procession to the Cathedral for the Divine Service and later joined in with the Celebrations of the laying of the foundation stone for the new triumphal arch at Bishop's Gate.

In the closing decades of the 18th century, the military quartered in Londonderry joined with the Apprentice Boys Companies, the

Blue Volunteers, the Volunteers Companies, the Liberty Volunteers, the Londonderry Legion and the Yeomen Cavalry and Infantry in commemorating the two historic anniversaries. Among these were the Londonderry Artillery (1783), the 13th Regiment (then the Somerset Light Infantry (Prince Albert's) (1786)), the 16th Regiment (then the Bedfordshire and Hertfordshire Regiment (1787)); the 46th Regiment (then the Duke of Cornwall's Light Infantry (1788)), the 28th Regiment (now the 1st Battalion The Duke of Gloucestershire Regiment (1789)), the 48th Regiment (then the 1st Battalion The Northamptonshire Regiment (1790)), the Fifeshire Fencibles (1795), the Royal Manx Fencibles (1796), the Londonderry Cavalry (1796), the Garrison and Infantry Cavalry (1797), the Breadalbane Fencibles (1798), and the Tipperary Militia (1798).

On 7th December 1797, Brigadier-General the Earl of Cavan, in a compliment to the citizens, ordered out the garrison, the artillery firing 21 rounds and the cavalry and infantry 3 volleys. In 1789, on the anniversary of the Shutting of the Gates the Londonderry Legion, who took part in the commemoration, were presented with a pair of colours by the Mayor of Corporation, John Darcus.

In the early years of the 19th century the Londonderry Yeomen Infantry and Rifle Company, together with the military, celebrated the Maiden City's two memorable days. The City of Dublin Militia and the Scots Greys joined with the Yeomanry in 1808 in commemorating the Relief. When the Lord Lieutenant, the Duke of Richmond, visited Londonderry in 1811, the loyal Apprentice Boys had the Red/Crimson flag, emblem of the Virgin City, repaired and displayed on the Cathedral. Often on anniversary occasions early in the 19th century, Sir George Hill and the Reverend John Graham led the Apprentice Boys on horseback, the latter riding a white steed.

Through the sheer determination and zeal from Siege descendants, the 18th of December Celebration was now firmly fixed in the calendar of the Apprentice Boys of Derry Association.

CHAPTER 2
THE LUNDY BUILDERS

For those unfamiliar with the stories surrounding the Siege of Derry 1688-89, it is important to explain that in popular history Colonel Robert Lundy has always been regarded as a traitor. The oral history passed down through generations has led to the tradition of burning an effigy of Lundy, depicted as a traitor, on 18th December every year.

As to who built the first effigy of Colonel Robert Lundy for the Shutting of the Gates Celebrations in 1788, this remains something of a mystery. Whilst we have some information about their status in society, it is not until we reach the 19th century onwards that we are on a firmer footing as to their identity.

The year 1788 remains the earliest recorded account about the building and burning of Lundy. The information was found in a Secular issued just after the 1788 Celebrations. This Secular states that the first Lundy effigy was made by the lower-class citizens of the City. Why the lower classes built the Lundy effigy in the first place remains something of a mystery. Were they trying to make some kind of a political statement, or were the scars of Lundy's treachery still so deeply rooted in the hearts of the Siege descendants that this simple act of pageantry was but a timely reminder for all who would seek to betray their hard-won Protestant freedom by displaying liberal attitudes in the face of adversity?

The Secular Commemoration, printed at the time, suggests that there was a good spirit of solidarity displayed at the Shutting of the Gates Celebrations in 1788. Both Roman Catholic and Protestant clergy of all denominations took part in the procession, along with the City's Dignitaries, to the Siege Cathedral for the Service of Thanksgiving. Later that day, they sat down together for a plain but plentiful dinner in the Town Hall. Whilst a spirit of solidarity between the church and state seems to have been present, this does not imply that the masses who had gathered in the City for the Celebrations were in total agreement. John Hempton in his book on the *Siege and History of Londonderry* states:

> "*This little bit of pageantry afforded no small entertainment to innumerable spectators, nor was it barren of instruction to an attentive mind, as it marked out, in striking characters, the unavoidable destiny of Traitors – who, having sacrificed to their own base interests, the dearest rights and honour and conscience, are deservedly consigned over to perpetual infamy, and become everlasting objects of detestation and derision even to the meanest of the people.*"[6]

Simpson in his book *The Annals of Derry* also writes that *"others"* saw the hanging and burning of the Lundy effigy in King William's Square as *"the objectionable part of the day's performance."*[7] There can be little doubt that the objectors were well aware of who the lower classes were getting at and

---

6   Hempton, John. *The Siege and History of Londonderry* (1861) p 82
7   Simpson, Robert. *The Annals of Derry* (1987) p 182

that this kind of pageantry was not welcomed as part of the Celebrations in developing good relationships within the City.

Among the personalities of influence in the City during this period of history was the notable Earl Bishop of Derry, Dr Frederick Hervey, who had made such an impact in the City. He had established and continued to develop good links with the entire City's clergy. From his own pocket he gave a substantial sum of £200 to the building of the Long Tower Church in 1784, and pacified the Presbyterians by helping fund some of their building projects. The Earl Bishop was also no stranger to frequently airing his strong political views, which caused all sorts of political turmoil in both Ireland and England. The appointment of the Bishop to the rank of Colonel of the Londonderry Corps of Volunteers raised some political concerns in both Ireland and in England as to where his true loyalties lay (See Appendix 1).

On the evening of 7th December 1788, a civic dinner was held in the Bishop's honour, but the Bishop was on vacation in Bordeauxeven, France. His absence seems to indicate that not all relationships within the City were good and that his absence was planned on purpose. The *Volunteer Evening Post* on 5th November 1784 portrayed a caricature of the Earl Bishop resembling that of Guy Fawkes, with the caption on the pedestal inscribed 'The Irish Patriot'. It is possible that it was this caricature of the Bishop that first inspired some of disgruntled citizens to make a Lundy effigy, a reminder to all who are in a position of authority and leadership that compromising religious and political beliefs, especially to those of a strong faith following Protestant traditions, is often considered nothing less than an act of treason.

Lundy effigies in the 19th and 20th centuries have also been viewed as a reminder to those in political and religious positions that treason to an important cause will not be tolerated.

In 1829-30 there was a large rat suspended from the wrist of Lundy, sending a clear message to those considered to be the political rats of the local Council and beyond. In December 1969 members of the General Committee of the Apprentice Boys of Derry, were called '*Lundys*', because for the first time in the history of the Association, they decided to uphold the Government's official ban on all parades and outdoor assemblies. This caused a split in the Association. Some members displayed the spirit of the Brave Thirteen, defied the ban and burned an effigy of Lundy at the junction of Hawkin Street and Fountain Street at approximately 4 pm (the usual time of the burning of Lundy on Walker's Pillar), despite the Army presence at the top of Hawkin Street. Some members of the General Committee who lived in the Fountain area, as they were making their way home from the Service in the Cathedral, passed the burning effigy of Lundy where they were greeted by angry locals who likened them to the Siege traitor. A hasty retreat was made by them, otherwise they too may well have succumbed to Lundy's fate.

While the traditional burning of Lundy has over the years developed into a more respectful historical occasion and less political, the local historical narratives as to why Lundy was burnt in the first place comprised of stories like; '*He was so hungry that he was going to sell the keys of the City Gates to King James for a bap,*' or that '*He was secretly a Roman Catholic at heart and a staunch supporter of King James II.*' The reality is that the historical Lundy effigy would always remain a subtle reminder to all that hard-won liberties must not to be compromised or diluted at any price.

There are no descriptive records of how the Lundy of 1788 was attired. Presumably, he must have had some sort of military attire on for the people to recognise him, and some kind of placard must have been hung around his neck for the population to label him Lundy! What we do know is that this first Lundy was made of tarred shavings and was full of gunpowder, and he was suspended from some kind of pole and burned at the eastern end of the Town Hall in King William's Square (The Diamond). Lundy's place of execution was moved from King William's Square to Walker's Pillar on the City walls in 1842; offering clear visibility to all who had gathered on the walls and beyond to witness the burning. This new location for Lundy's burning also added further insult to the Lundy effigy, in that he would be executed beneath the feet of Reverend George Walker, the Siege hero of 1688/89.

The first but brief description on what the Lundy effigy looked like is recorded in the *Londonderry Journal* in 1822:

> *"The traitor Lundy was suspended from a gallows in the Diamond, bearing on his shoulders the usual bundle of faggots, and decorated with the novel appendages of a pair of mustachios, and on the seat of honour, a bunch of leeks."*

There he hung dangling in the wind from a gibbet until the time of burning which was late in the afternoon, which amused a large crowd of people who had gathered there for his burning.

Two characteristic features emerge from this brief description of the Lundy effigy, which became part of the norm in Lundy-building right up to this present day, i.e., the bundle of faggots on his back and the thick black mustachios. The faggots placed on the shoulders of Lundy is a misunderstanding of the term 'match'. Tow, or match, was used to fire matchlock muskets, and Lundy in his escape is said to have carried a bundle of match on his shoulders as a means to disguise himself as he fled from the City. In the passage of time this match was misinterpreted to mean matchwood for a fire, which explains why the effigy of Lundy has a bundle of faggots or scallops on his back. As to the thick black mustachios, its meaning is unknown. As there are no images of him to verify this, maybe the Colonel actually had one. People also speculate that the Lundy builders may have taken liberties in putting one on Lundy's face, or maybe the facial features of the effigy portrayed some political figure in the City who people were disgruntled with.

The Apprentice Boys of Derry Organisation by 1814 was now in a much stronger position than it had been since its infancy in 1772, and began to take a more active role in the Siege Celebrations as the military role decreased. It is plausible that it was also during this period of transition that the organisation took upon itself the responsibility for building the early Lundy effigies; after all, they were now the primary movers in ensuring that the Shutting of the Gates and the Relief of Derry Celebrations should never be forgotten.

A fuller description of the Lundy effigy and its progressive development is described for us in *The Londonderry Standard* in 1837. It states that:

> "It was quite a masterpiece in its way. The figure stood upwards of seven feet in height, was neatly proportioned about the bust as a merchant tailor's block. The costume was that of a military officer's dress (including a frock coat), with the exception of an immense cocked hat which might have been the property of a field-marshal, or a Lord Mayor's coachman. The legs were developed in a pair of undefinables

which would have provoked the envy of Count D'Orsay and which were drawn over a pair of exquisitely finished Wellington boots. On the breast of the figure was sewn a large placard, inscribed 'This is the end of all traitors', and on the back was another, inscribed 'Lundy the Traitor'. A bundle of faggots was fastened upon the shoulders and the whole traitor, in his airy attitude, as he kept twirling and salaaming to the multitude had more the air of a self-satisfied dandy with a kitchen clout at his tail, looking about him for applause in happy unconsciousness of his laughable appendage, than that of one whose infamous memory was deemed to an sternization of contempt. Indeed some of the wags have discovered in the effigy of the traitor a striking likeness of a certain popularity-loving chief governor, who is more than suspected of being one of the Lundy family. The features of his face were of a delicate pale green, surmounted by a thatch of curls, which certainly did not look exactly as if they had just left the hands of a first-rate Parisian friseur. The eyes were like the eyes of a half-boiled haddock, looking for all the world as if they had been born in the middle of the week, each looking out for Sunday. The mouth - oh! ye gods, what a mouth! The only redeeming feature was the tongue, which was a cut from a slice of raw beef-steak, and lolled out of the mouth against the cadaverous cheek with a sort of seriocomic expression towards the crowd, as if scoffing at them with reckless impunity."

The effigy was then suspended from a pole by means of a pulley and rope which projected out of one of the east windows of the Town Hall. The identity of the builders of this Lundy still remains a mystery.

In 1862, the Treasurer of the Murray Club of the Apprentice Boys of Derry Club was ordered to pay £1 towards the cost of building the effigy

Some of the early Lundy builders. Right to Left. The man in the soft hat is Johnny Holland to his left is Matthew Kerr the Governor of the Apprentice Boys of Derry Association. Standing to the left of the Governor, is Andy Cresswell and the young man standing behind the man with the stick to light Lundy is Young Bobby Jackson. The three men standing at the back, to the far right, is Bobby Jackson Sen. This photograph was taken in the forties.

Three generations of Jackson Lundy Builders.

of Colonel Lundy. Mr Thomas Irvine (who was Vice President of the Murray Club in 1869, and in all probability a brother of the first President of the Club, David Irvine) was appointed to assist in the making of the effigy. It would seem that in those early days it was the responsibility of the various Apprentice Boys Clubs to not only pay for the effigy making, but also assist or make the effigy themselves. This is not a new development, but something that still exists to the present day, i.e. each Apprentice Boys Club will take it in turn to fund the constructing of the effigy, but not necessarily take an active part in its construction. This is a task that is given to a select few – namely the Lundy builders, who are usually members of the Apprentice Boys Association, but not necessary from the same Club.

In 1842, fire-crackers were placed in the centre of the main body of the effigy, providing a colourful display which amused the crowds who gathered to watch the burning of Lundy on the City walls. The tradition of placing fireworks inside the Lundy effigy continued up to 1968, which was the last year in which Lundy was burned on Walker's pillar. The chief reason for the disuse of fireworks as part of the 18th Celebrations was the outbreak of the Troubles, as they could easily be mistaken for gunfire. This bit of pageantry and fun has never been replaced nor could it ever have been reintroduced, given the various locations where Lundy was burned.

The first time the location of where the Lundy Effigy was built is recorded in 1844. It was constructed in the Apprentice Boys Club Room in Linen Hall. At six o'clock in the morning of the 18th, the Lundy effigy was carried up the walls to Walker's Pillar. The construction of the Lundy effigy between 1862 until the opening of the new Apprentice Boys of Derry Association Hall in Society Street in 1877 could have occurred at several locations, the obvious being the old Town Hall in the Diamond, as this is where Lundy was burned until his new location in 1832. Another possible location was Foy's old coach factory, which stood on part of the site of the present-day Apprentice Boys Memorial Hall, and which was used occasionally by the Murray Club for its meetings. The Lundy effigy could even have been built at the Old School Rooms in Pump Street, as they too were used by various Apprentice Boys Clubs for Club meetings, or even the Club Room located on Church Wall.

Provision for an area to build Lundy was created in the old boiler room in the basement of the Old Apprentice Boys of Derry Memorial Hall (built in 1877). In the current Apprentice Boys Club Room, prior to the replacement of the old wooden floor, there were two trap doors located in the centre of the room. The purpose of these trap doors was to enable the Lundy builders to stand the effigy upright so that he could be dressed in his military uniform, where he would remain hanging until the evening of the 17th. Once Lundy was swilled with ropes, it would then be drawn up through the trap doors into the Club Room and placed on two wooden trestles until the dawning of the 18th morning, then it would then be carried off to Walker's Pillar, hung up and burned later in the day.

By 1875, the task of building Lundy was given to Hugh Sheppard and Thomas Cabena (both members of the Apprentice Boys Association). Thomas Cabena owned a small joiner's shop in London Street (beside the Talk of the Town pub) and it was his pulleys and wire ropes that were used to hoist Lundy up on Walker's Pillar for the December Celebrations. Local publications around this time give us a clear picture of how the effigy looked. It stood approximately 14 feet, was dressed in something to resemble a military uniform, coloured black. Two placards were placed on it. The one on the front read 'Lundy The Traitor' and the one fixed on its back read, 'The End Of All Traitors'. A bundle of faggots was also tied around the back of its shoulders. This effigy was likely to have been stuffed with the same substance as in previous years, which was a mixture of pitch, turpentine and resin. In 1842 fire-crackers were placed in the centre of the main body of the effigy, providing a colourful display.

Mr James Wilton is mentioned as being main builder of the effigy from 1885 to 1902. Other members of the Wilton family would have helped in the building of Lundy. James Wilton's Lundy effigy stood about fifteen feet in stature, had fine rosy cheeks and a well-trimmed beard. Its smile was rigid with a trace of cynicism. The face of the effigy had openings at the eyes and at the mouth. It was adorned with a large cock-hat, white gloves, a tailed-coat, waist-coat and boots that measured two feet and six inches long. On the front of the effigy's chest was a large placard, with the inscription 'Lundy The Traitor,' and on the back it read, 'The End Of All Traitors'. Underneath this outer uniform, the effigy had a framework of wire. This was placed around the whole of the effigy, which helped to keep the structure together when it was burning from Walker's Pillar. The Wiltons also placed the usual bundle of scallops on its back and filled it with fireworks. The crowds enjoyed watching the display whilst the effigy was burning.

What emerges from this more detailed description of Lundy construction is that old electrical wire was now being used to keep the whole framework together. Prior to this, the burning effigy would have fallen quite rapidly after being set alight, which proved to be dangerous for spectators close to the base of the Pillar and those watching it burn from Naylor's Row, situated below Walker's Pillar. The description of cutting holes in the face suggest that it was well constructed from papier mâché, allowing fireworks to be placed in both eyes and in his mouth for greater effect. The large beard was some kind of horse hair, dyed black and stuck to the face with glue. The height of the effigy is also worth noting, in that it would have looked substantial when hung on the Pillar, a larger than life character.

James Wilton's brother, David, took on the family mantel of building Lundy in 1902 and was ably assisted by Mr David Norrie (better known as wee Dickie). Mr Dickie Norrie was small in stature and was the Caretaker of the Apprentice Boys of Derry Memorial Hall in Society Street. In this same year Dickie Norrie was elected as Secretary to the Murray Parent Club, where he was recorded as being methodical in his role as Club Secretary. Mr David Norrie would carry on the Lundy building tradition up to 1926. While Dickie followed the Wilton's pattern, it was said that his Lundy was much smaller in size and that Dickie would often be seen with the Lundy effigy tucked under his arm as he made his way onto Derry walls and toward Walker's Pillar on the 18th morning. Mr Dickie Norrie was the first to design and make a cement mould for the making of Lundy's face. This same mould was passed to the Wilton family and then to Mr Robert Jackson Senior and was last used in 1985, when Robert Jackson Junior along with other members of his family made their last Lundy for the Apprentice Boys of Derry Association. This mould and two other Lundy moulds, remain the private property of the Jackson family.

Significant changes took take place in 1927. Mr Dickie Norrie had retired from making the Lundy and now a new Lundy team of builders began to emerge. This new team consisted of Andrew White (better known as Andy), who won an MC and a MM during the Great War of 1914-18; James Hamilton (whose small cannon used for ushering in the 18th morning was confiscated by the police after it was fired on the City walls in 1929); W Carson (better known as 'Knotty', a small stout man and a joiner by trade who made the wooden soles for the boots); and then there was the late R Jackson Senior better known as 'Bobby' of 3 Clarence Place, Fountain Street.

Together this team redesigned the whole Lundy structure. Among the changes that were made was the replacing of traditional swale tail-coat with a large black frock-coat (a tradition that continues up to this present day). The traditional breeches and stockings were replaced by straight black trousers, saving both time and material. The Lundy was wired from head to foot in mesh-wire as a safety precaution, preventing any injury to the crowd during the burning from Walker's Pillar, as in December it could be very windy.

The effigy now stood at sixteen feet tall and was almost a ton in weight. It was stuffed with wood shavings and had plenty of fire-rockets placed in it, which caused great effect while he burned on the Pillar. Lundy's boots were made up of two parts; a wooden sole with black leather uppers which formed the shape of the foot and upper boot, with a second sole that had a heel and was studded with nails. The overall length of Lundy's boots measured three feet, and the outer studded part of the boot was often given as a souvenir to the individual who had the honour of lighting the effigy that year. Lundy's traditional cock-hat remained. This was made out of strong cardboard purchased from Davan's Box Factory, situated in Aubery Street, off Wapping Lane. Further additions to Lundy's uniform were the introduction of two black painted epaulettes by Bobby Jackson Senior. The pattern for these was drawn up by Bernard's of the Strand Road, who specialised in making military and naval uniforms.

Black oilcloth buttons became part of the uniform and were placed down the front of the frock-coat in two rows and one at each corner of the placards/bills. (The bills were printed by the Londonderry Sentinel Office in Pump Street.) The white coloured face of the effigy with a huge black

Lily Jackson, Bobby's wife applies the light to Lundy December 1967.

moustache was still made by the Wilton family right up into the 1940s and the two white gloves that he wore had painted fingernails on them.

The Lundy effigy in the early 1930s became more elegant in its structure and more colourful than that of the 1920s. A new team of Lundy builders had new ideas about its appearance, and each of them being experts in their own respective trades brought that expertise to good use in constructing the effigy. Among those now responsible for making the effigy were Mr Noble Ferguson and Mr Andy White, (who supervised the whole construction), Mr James Hamilton, Mr J C Thompson, and Mr Bobby Jackson Senior. Sometime in the mid-1930s, James Hamilton took on the responsibility for supervising the building of Lundy aided by Knotty Carson and Bobby Jackson Senior, but James Hamilton only took charge of this task for one year. Following this, Knotty Carson took full charge of building the Lundy and was aided by Mr Noble Ferguson, (who was an upholsterer by trade and made the military uniform for the Lundy), Bobby Jackson Senior (a coach painter by trade as well as being a part-time Fire Officer at Duke Street Fire Station, who was later responsible for painting the uniform for Lundy), along with Mr Bob Young and Mr Noble Divine. The latter were upholsterers by trade and they dressed the Lundy in his military uniform. It was often said that both men always had a mouthful of needles and would quite happily chew on them when at work on the effigy, and to engage with them in conversation was not always advisable!

The Lundy that these men made stood sixteen feet tall, four feet across the chest, twenty-eight inches around the neck and weighed fifteen hundredweight. The cock-hat from tip to tip was four feet long and eighteen inches deep and was now trimmed with a yellow band around its edge. The gloves were twenty-eight inches long by twelve inches wide. In all, thirty-six yards of material was required to makes its clothes. Lundy's boots were twenty-eight and a half inches long by eleven and a half inches wide. They were studded with 137 nails, (in 1931 the number of nails used, had increased to 150), all arranged as if in a real pair of boots. The upper part of its boots, were made by Harpers of Duke Street and the soles were made by Balintine's of the Strand Road (later called E Key's). While the whole structure of the Lundy was changed in terms of size and additional new bits of uniform added, the effigy still did not have any colour added to its uniform. In fact, the only redeeming feature was the large white face with a moustache and a rocket placed at the side of his mouth, sticking out like a cigar. The two white gloves and the two white bills/placards with large black lettering on them, helped to break up this huge black figure. Even the lapels and pockets were black and could only been seen on close inspection of the effigy. It was not until the late 1930s or early 1940s that colour was introduced to Lundy's uniform.

Mr Bobby Jackson Senior in the early 1940s introduced two new traditions around the burning of Lundy. He suggested that the soles (the studded part of the boots) be taken off the Lundy before he was set on fire and that one of them should be given as a souvenir to the person who had the honour of lighting the Lundy effigy and the other to the President of the Club which had paid for Lundy's construction. Secondly, that an elegant turned wooden touch (stick), beautifully painted, lined and inscribed be presented to the one given the task of lighting Lundy on the day. As Bobby Jackson was a coach painter by trade, he got the task of painting the touch, as well as painting the presentation inscription on the soles of Lundy's boots.

Such was the pride that these Lundy builders took in their work, that they produced an effigy that was to become the flagship for all other

Lundy builders in Northern Ireland to follow. It is said that when the Lundy effigy was hoisted up on Walker's Pillar at 6.30 am, that they would stand back and admire their handiwork, salute the effigy with a bottle of stout and then march around the base of the Pillar singing *'We'll guard old Derry's Walls,'* all before the ringing of the Cathedral joy bells ushering in the 18th morning.

In another incident, in the late 1930s on the evening of the 18th Celebrations, Bobby's wife Lilly had just finished painting an old basket chair and placed it near the fire to dry in their house. Some of Bobby's friends from the Apprentice Boys Association (Mr Connor and the Finlay brothers, the latter being explosive experts) called and insisted that Bobby have a few drinks with them in his house. Mr Connor sat in Lilly's newly painted chair with his new raincoat on, oblivious to the fact that it wasn't dry and they all happily sang and drank until it almost reached midnight. The Finlay brothers said that they should all make their way over to the walls, and Bobby Junior went over with them. On their arrival at the Royal Bastion, the Finlay brothers said to Bobby that the large cannon nearest the flagpole was cleaned out and loaded by them during the day and was ready for firing. At first no one would believe them, but they insisted that it was so. After much dialogue they entered the bastion, young Bobby was given a touch stick and as the Guildhall clock struck twelve midnight, he followed their instructions, touched the firing point, and the cannon fired sending out a flame of approximately eighteen feet long and spraying paper all over Nailor's Row like wedding confetti. Young Bobby was blown off his feet and suffered hearing loss for several months. Bobby Senior, the Findlay brothers and Connor marched around the base of Walker's Pillar singing *'Derry Walls'* and *'The Sash'*. It remains a mystery how they were not arrested for their actions or that no one was seriously hurt. For them, The Day had truly started off with a bang!

The outbreak of the Second World War had a significant impact on the 18th Celebrations. It was impossible to get the black material to make Lundy's uniform due to the demand for blackout material to shut out light in the evenings and prevent the City from being bombed by the German Luftwaffe. The Lundy builders found themselves having to improvise by using brown sacking material, which was covered with lampblack dye. This left a terrible mess on the floor of the Lundy's Room. In fact, the floor of this room still had the outline of two boots on the wooden floor up until 1985. The lampblack dye was very effective, but disaster struck in one particular year when heavy rain began to fall on the effigy swaying in the wind from Walker's Pillar. The dye started to run on what was essentially a colourful and well-constructed effigy, reducing it to a large black ghastly figure of a man.

With the new extension added to the existing Apprentice Boys of Derry Memorial Hall in 1938, a special room had been designed for the sole purpose of building Lundy. Even today this room is still referred to as 'Lundy's Room'. It was rectangular in shape and had high ceilings. This made it an ideal room for building and dressing the effigy with ease, as well as providing a space where people could just pop in, to see and talk to the Lundy builders at work. This room was also fitted with a fire hose in case the unthinkable took place. Any slighting comments about the shape or the uniform of the Lundy effigy meant disagreements could arise if the individual did not quickly remove themselves from Lundy's room!

By the late 1940s and into the early 1950s, colour was now applied to the uniform of Lundy.

The large cock-hat had a two-inch strip painted around its edge with three yellow frills attached to it, which hung down. One of them was placed in the centre of the hat at the top and the other two at either ends. The large black frock-coat had a row of three yellow buttons on each sleeve, and six yellow buttons were placed around Lundy's two white bills. Two broad yellow strips were painted down each side of his trousers, and two yellow painted epaulettes added to the shoulders. Lundy's face remained as colourful as ever. However, some things did not change. Lundy still had two black lapels, which remained unnoticeable to the naked eye; and although two new cuffs were introduced to finish off Lundy's sleeves, they resulted in a waste of black material as no one could see them unless they were up close. The effigy was now usually built approximately seventeen feet in height and weighed almost a ton.

The team had now been reduced to a handful of dedicated men who devoted themselves to making sure that the 18th December Celebrations would not be minus an effigy of Colonel Robert Lundy to burn from Walker's Pillar. Among the Lundy builders was Mr J (Joey) Ferguson, who was the grandson of Mr Noble Ferguson, and Mr John (Jonny) Holland of Kennedy Street, Wapping Lane. Both of these men were upholsters by trade and they both worked in Hills of the Strand Road. Their role was to dress the effigy in its military uniform, and on more than one occasion tempers would flare between them and other members of the team about how the uniform should look on the standing effigy. Mr Robert Jackson Senior and Robert Junior (the two Bobby's), did most of the actually stuffing of the effigy, as well as painting Lundy's uniform. Mr Andrew (Andy) Cresswell worked as a van driver for the Londonderry Gas Company, and it was he who supervised the construction of Lundy for the Celebrations. Andy Cresswell's period of building Lundy came to an abrupt end, when on a stormy 18th December day, he climbed up onto the base of Walker's Pillar (against the strong advice of others present), to try and tie a rope around Lundy's legs to keep him from swaying all over the place. The Lundy swung round and hit Andy, knocking him off the base onto the concrete ground below. Andy was taken to the City and County Hospital, where he survived the fall but his Lundy building days were now over.

Through death and old age this team of Lundy builders was further reduced until only two of the original five were left to build it, namely Bobby Jackson Senior and Bobby Junior. They already had a long-standing track record of building Lundy in the City, as well as one for Belfast and Donemana and it was the obvious choice that they should be the ones to carry on with this building tradition. Having gained a vast amount of experience in Lundy building they introduced change from the very start. No more would they try to sew Lundy's hair on to the back of his head while he was lying on his back, getting mattress stuffing in their eyes during the whole process. Nor would they try to fit his arms and frock-coat simultaneously while the effigy was standing up, working from ladders seventeen feet high. They had observed the previous struggle when an even easier way had been suggested and it had been quickly dismissed because 'this is how it was always done!' Various traders in the City also had a role to play in producing Lundy's clothing. The wooden soles for its boots were made in Balintine's in the Strand Road by a man called Picket. The epaulettes were made by Bernard's Military Outfitters of the Strand Road, who produced the pattern for Mr Bobby Jackson Senior in the late 1920s. The upper parts of Lundy's boots were made by Harpers of Duke Street. The Londonderry Sentinel Office printed the two large white bills, and both colours of sacking which made up the uniform were purchased from Hills of the Strand Road.

The Jackson family (most of their members were now involved in building Lundy) took over building Lundy in 1958 and Mr Busty Wilton gave Bobby Jackson the cement mould that he used for making Lundy's face, as he had no further need of it. The Londonderry Sentinel Office had also ceased to print the two white bills that Lundy wore on his chest and back, from now on it was going to be a family responsibility to construct and dress the City's effigy.

The Jacksons kept their promise to make a bigger, more colourful and simplified effigy of Robert Lundy, unlike the more completed versions of earlier years. This new design was to become the personal hallmark of the Jackson family and to some extent is still used today.

Now the Lundy effigy stood a full eighteen feet, was seven foot across the chest and weighed a ton. When fully constructed and laying on his back, it was a tight squeeze for anyone to get past his arms up to his head. People often had to crawl on all fours under him to get to the top of his head. Lundy's cock-hat was made much bigger and retained all the usual trimmings. His frock-coat had a broad yellow strip down the front of the coat and a fancy swirling design at the back of the coat just below the white bill, which branched off into two yellow strips fishing off at the bottom of the coat about two feet apart. For the first time ever, the two black pockets, which were often unnoticed, were lined in yellow around three sides making them more obvious to the eye of the beholder. A further distinguishing feature was the high stand-up collar, which was yellow lined with a design painted in the centre of it. This was to replace the usual two black lapels, which again to the untrained eye remained unseen by the public when Lundy was hoisted up on Walker's Pillar. In addition to all of the other changes, the Jackson family made the uppers of Lundy's boots and included approximately ten eyelets, so that his boots could be properly laced up like any normal pair of shoes. The laces on Lundy's boots often amused visitors to the Apprentice Boys Memorial Hall, who called to view the Lundy before the Big Day. School children were fascinated by these boots and some even believed that he had laced them himself prior to their visit to Lundy's Room. What had not changed was the brightly coloured hand painted face, the two yellow epaulettes, the two strips down the outer part of his trousers, the large white gloves and the two large bills (hand painted by Bobby Senior) fastened by eight yellow buttons on each bill.

It took fifty ten-stone bags of wood shavings (mainly gathered from Keys timber yard of the Strand Road) and between £10 and £15-worth of rockets to construct the main body of the effigy. Used for the first time, at least two full rolls of fine chicken wire were required to wrap around Lundy's main body. Several bags of old electrical wire, gathered from several electrical shops in the City, were wrapped around the chicken wire, keeping the whole body tight and attached to the main metal backbone of Lundy. Twenty yards of brown hessian sacking was required to make the main body of the effigy, including its two arms. Thirty-five yards of black cloth was required to make its uniform, five yards of white material was needed to make his two bills and white gloves. One ball of white cord was used to sew the unseen bits of the body together and two spools of black harness thread was used to sew the uniform on the effigy. Two gallons of white and yellow paint were needed to paint stripes on the uniform, plus two boxes of half-inch tacks for studding the soles of Lundy's boots. Four yards of rexene was used to make the two epaulettes and the remainder of this material made up the two uppers of Lundy's boots. Several sewing needles were needed for the family Singer pedal sewing machine. Lundy's hat was initially made from cardboard, but this often got torn from Lundy's head on stormy days when he was hanging from the Pillar. Stiff oil-cloth was a second option, which proved to be the best material to make the hat so it remained rigid even in strong winds. All of the sewing of Lundy's clothes was done by Bobby Senior's wife, Lily, then his daughters Ruby and Daphne and lastly, Bobby Junior's wife, Kathleen. These ladies spent hours making Lundy's clothes and many a dispute broke out if some part of the uniform was sewn incorrectly. The women were as dedicated to making the Lundy effigy a success as the men who constructed it.

While no official pattern existed for the making of Lundy, those involved in his building knew what size he needed to be and in order to make sure that he would be right in terms of his proportion, his clothes were measured out and cut to size on the floor in Lundy's room at the Apprentice Boys Memorial Hall. The painted work on Lundy's uniform started about mid-September in Bobby Jackson Senior's shed at the bottom of Clarence Place. There he would design the pattern to be painted on the two sleeves of Lundy's frock-coat, the pockets, the cock-hat, the two studded soles, plus the touch stick to light the effigy on the 18th and the large papier mâché face. These bits of uniform once painted, would be often seen hanging on large flagpoles in his shed or from the indoor pulley creel on the staircase of Bobby's house. People had to be agile on the stairs at Bobby's house to ensure that they wouldn't brush against the painted uniform and get paint on their own clothes. There was always an air of excitement in 3 Clarence Place when younger family members saw Lundy's clothes hanging about the place. It meant that it would not be too long before they actually started to build the effigy for the big day.

Building a Lundy consisted of three stages:

The first stage was usually the hardest, the dirtiest, but usually the most enjoyable. There was the stuffing of the brown hessian sacking, which made up Lundy's main body. Lundy's backbone was a seven-foot-long iron bar that was round at the top end, where the cock-hat was positioned and tapered off to a flat area. There were three main areas on this backbone. The first one was the main area to which the brown sacking was attached and which made up the torso of the Lundy. This sacking was tacked onto two four feet long by four inches thick boards that were bolted in four areas to the majority of the flatted backbone. To make sure that the sacking did not tear away from the two boards when stuffed, a broad strip of oilcloth was tacked over the sacking to secure it in place. At the bottom end of the backbone was a longer bolt that had spacers on either side of the main backbone. Attached to this were two thirteen foot long, by six inches wide, by two and a half inch boards, which helped to shape Lundy's two legs and to which his boots were attached. At the top end of the backbone was a small cross bolt, over which the head sacking was pulled, which formed the head of the Lundy. The remainder of the top of the backbone accommodated the cock-hat, leaving a ring at the top, where the pulley hook was attached, enabling the effigy to be hosted up into position for dressing and burning.

Once Lundy's backbone had been prepared, it was fastened to the wooden floor at the top two corners by two tacks. This kept the chest area of Lundy from moving all over the place while it was being filled with shavings, wooden blocks and fireworks. Once the torso was stuffed to capacity, the brown hessian trousers were pulled over the two wooden boards and attached to the main trunk of the effigy. Again, a lot of hard work had to be put in to filling the two legs so that they went completely round the wooden boards fixed in the middle of the stuffed legs. This first process could take up to two or three nights to complete, sometimes longer. All of the sewing that had to be done at this stage was done using brown parcel cord and long twisty needles. All those involved, no matter how young they were, had the opportunity to develop their sewing skills and have a good bit of fun in the process. During these evenings, the Jackson family along with other interested individuals would discuss and debate incidents related to the Siege of Derry, especially Lundy's role in it. Stories were told of how Lundy was so hungry during the Siege that he had reached the position that he was willing to surrender keys of the City to King James' army for a bap (a bun or a bread roll). Or that he escaped from the City disguised as a wood cutter by climbing down a pear tree at Orchard Street, with a load of match wood on his back, and eventually made his escape to London. Other stories and oral history were related about the good old days of Lundy making, the men who made him and about how events had changed the programme of the 18th Celebrations over the past years.

The second stage of the construction of the effigy was a lot more laborious. It involved in getting the effigy ready for hanging up to be dressed in his military uniform. This second stage commenced with the application of chicken mesh wire to the whole body area of the Lundy effigy. In order to keep this chicken mesh wire in place and to keep the whole-body structure of the Lundy together, strands of electrical wire were wrapped around the torso and legs of the effigy. Once this had been done, several main electrical wires were run from the bottom of the Lundy's legs right the whole way up to the top of his body and attached to the main backbone. These long strands of wire was interwoven through the electrical wires that were placed around Lundy's chest and legs. When this interweaving had had been completed, the effigy structure was now more solid and manageable so it could be moved back and forth as required. While this part of the Lundy building was boring, it was a safety necessity as it kept the whole structure together when it was burning and it kept the watching public safe.

When the wiring of the Lundy had been completed, the next step was to fix in place the head and shoulder sacking over the top of the backbone (iron bar) and sew it in place at the top of Lundy's torso. This was stuffed with wood shavings, later straw. (Straw was introduced in the early 1970s and was supplied by Mr Tommy Craig, a farmer from the Drumahoe area who was a member of the Browning Club. The straw was introduced due to the difficulty of obtaining wood shavings.) With the shoulder section shaped, the whole Lundy was soaked through with cold water from the fire hose in Lundy's room. The reason for doing this was to allow the wood shavings or straw to swell, making the whole Lundy fit tight against the chicken mesh wire. This procedure usually happened on Friday evening as it allowed the Lundy to dry out over the weekend ready for the final part of this second stage in Lundy building. This was pulling on the dress trousers and nailing the upper part of Lundy's boots to the two wooden legs attached to the lower part of the backbone.

Now the effigy was ready for hanging up in the highest part of Lundy's room, which was approximately 22 feet high, so there was no room for error in the height Lundy needed to be. This hoisting usually took place when there was either an Apprentice Boys Club or Orange Order meeting taking place, as it provided the manpower to help hoist Lundy up into an upright position. It was hard and was not without its dangers, especially to the one who was at the top end of Lundy's room pulling on the block and tackle chain. Once in place there was often a sigh of relief by the Lundy builders that everything had gone according to plan. Lundy was now ready for the third stage.

This third stage of Lundy's construction started with the fitting of its two arms, these were attached to the main body by wire and then sewn into place. Once secure, the two large white gloves were sewn into place at the end of each arm. Lundy's large black frock coat was the next thing to be fitted and sewn in place, followed by the two black sleeves with yellow painted cuffs. The face, hair and hat were the next items to be fitted into place followed by more elaborate parts of the uniform, the two yellow lined pockets, two yellow epaulets, upright collar and the two large white bills ('Lundy The Traitor' on the front and 'The End Of All Traitors' on its back), edged with eight large yellow buttons made out of oil cloth.

Now that the effigy was complete, it remained upright in Lundy's Room until the eve of his demise. The night before his burning the Lundy effigy had to be bound up with a long thick rope. Its purpose was twofold. Firstly, it kept the arms and legs tight together making it easier to manoeuvre Lundy about, especially when it came to lowering him down and placing him on his large wooden table in the long narrow room. Secondly, it gave the men something to grip when it came to carrying Lundy out of his room and up onto the City walls towards Walker's Pillar. Once at the Pillar, the rope was removed and Lundy was hoisted up into place above the base of the Pillar. There it was fastened to its column by another rope to keep it from being destroyed by strong winds. While Lundy lay on the large wooden table, the two soles of his boots were nailed on – now the Lundy was complete and ready for the arrival of the big day. The revival of the Crimson Ball on the 17th evening provided an opportunity to add a bit more pageantry to the evening events. Firstly, there was the nailing on of Lundy's soles, an opportunity given to very few people (Judge Jones

QC and MP for the City of Londonderry along with his wife, Dr W R Abernethy OBE and his wife, and finally the Hon R Chichester-Clark MP and his wife). Later in the evening, both Bobby's would be down in Lundy's room by 11.30 pm to load the two small brass canons ready for firing the customary thirteen shots at midnight to usher in the Shutting of the Gates Celebrations.

Between the years 1969 and December 1971 there was a government ban on all parades. This was problematic for the Apprentice Boys of Derry Association in the City. What about the old tradition of the burning of Lundy? Unknown to the Apprentice Boys of Derry, a smaller version of Lundy was secretly made in accordance with the usual pattern. Ban or no ban, Lundy would still be built!

Towards the end of this particular family's history in building Lundy, the effigy's uniform became more elaborate in design and instead of just a broad yellow strip down the front of his coat; it was now elegantly designed with two lapels and a lace cravat. The cravat on Lundy was introduced by the Jackson family in the early 1970s and remained an iconic part of Lundy's uniform up to the last Lundy that this family made for the Apprentice Boys of Derry Organisation. This was in December 1985 after the death of Bobby Senior on the Easter Sunday of that same year. This last Lundy was made by Bobby Jackson Junior and his son William. Mrs Kathleen Jackson, Bobby's, wife did all the sewing for the effigy. Bobby's son Albert, who had been Chaplain to the Walker Parent Club, and who was studying for ministry, applied the torch to light the effigy.

This does not mean that the family had completely given up building Lundy effigies. A Lundy very similar in style to the last one burned in 1985 was displayed in the Kennedy Street area of the Fountain at the Tercentenary in August 1988. This effigy consisted of a large wooden frame on which the dress uniform was pulled over and fixed in place, giving the impression that it was a fully stuffed Lundy. A large metal bar across his chest at the upper part of the frame took the full weight of the effigy's body and arms. This bar rested on two metal brackets that were fitted to the upper part of the wall of the nursery school that was at the end of the new housing in Kennedy Street. Lundy stood the full eighteen feet and measured seven feet across the chest. In 1990 this effigy was displayed in the Ulster Folk and Transport Museum just outside Belfast for six months, in an exhibition celebrating various traditions from different communities. On its return to the City, it was given as a gift to the City Tower Museum as part of their permanent display. A smaller version of Lundy is still displayed in the upper part of the Fountain at the Relief of Derry Celebrations every year. This was made by the Jackson family, the last remaining members of the old Lundy builders of the Apprentice Boys of Derry Organisation. The Jackson family will forever be remembered by all who visit the Tower Museum in the City and all who are interested in the traditions and events connected the Shutting of the Gates Celebrations.

CHAPTER 3
WE'LL FIGHT AND NOT SURRENDER!

T G Fraser in his book *The Irish Parading Tradition*, states that there are five key issues that surround the Protestant parading traditions. They are: *"territory, tradition, cultural identity, civil rights and politics."*[8] Unlike the Orange Order, the Apprentice Boys of Derry Association did its very best to steer away from a political, dogmatic approach to celebrating the Siege of Londonderry, although there were a few occasions when it was on the brink of political involvement in Northern Ireland affairs, (one being during the rise and early political career of Reverend Ian Paisley who sought to drive home the message that Ulster would remain part of the United Kingdom, despite the betrayal of other Ulster politicians, better known as Lundys!).

The Apprentice Boys Constitution and Rule Book, and the Initiation Ceremony into the Organisation, clearly state that the reason for its existence is to perpetrate the Shutting of the Gates and the Relief of Derry in a manner that is acceptable to both sides of the community.

---

8 Fraser, T G. *The Irish Parading Tradition* (2000) p 6

It is not for political gain nor must it be seen as an organisation that demonstrates a triumphal attitude over Roman Catholics living in the City. The early Siege Celebrations were enjoyed by both sides of the community, who actively took part in the Celebrations. In 1788 and 1789, the Roman Catholic Bishop Dr McDevitt and other clergy of various religious traditions, joined the City Corporation with other dignitaries, a mixture of Volunteer forces, trade apprentices and merchants from the City. By all accounts, a spirit of equilibrium prevailed at the Celebrations, but this was not to last. Several factors have been suggested as to why this relationship was harmonious within the City. By the early 17th Century Roman Catholics began moving back into the City and its suburbs. A more liberal government in 1745 permitted the building of Roman Catholic Churches for worship. In 1784, Father Lynch oversaw the building of the Long Tower Church just outside the City walls on the old site of the ancient monastery of St Colmcille. Subscriptions for the building of the Long Tower Church were received from several benefactors, including the Earl Bishop who donated £200, the City Corporation gave £50, and several Protestant gentlemen from the parish of Glendermott who also helped build it through liberal subscriptions. Also the Catholic Relief Act of 1782 gave Catholics the same land rights as that of Protestants, and in September of that year, Father Lynch and Bishop McDevitt, the Dean and other clergy took the Oath of Allegiance to King George III. All of these factors helped pave the way for mutual respect and a greater understanding of people's cultural and religious traditions.

The rise of United Irishmen and the ensuing rebellion and uprising of 1798 did have an impact in the City. An estimated 80,000 United Irishmen were in Ulster in 1787, of that number 10,000 were in County Londonderry. A number of captured United Irishmen were publicly flogged in the City in full view of its citizens. The citizens of the City made a public rebuttal of the United Irishmen's action on 19th to 24th June 1778, which witnessed the greatest part of the County inhabitants voluntarily arrive in the City to take the Oath of Allegiance to the King. In July upwards of 1,000 people took the Oath before W H Ash Esq of Ashbrooke. Quite a number of those who made up those 1,000 persons, surrendered their pikes and other weaponry and many of them acknowledged that they had previously taken the Oath of the United Irishmen. The repercussion of what was happening in Ulster and especially in the County of Londonderry caused the citizens to declare that:

> "We resolve to form ourselves into a military corps, to be called the Londonderry Yeoman Infantry, and do agree, in addition to the oath prescribed by law, to take this declaration – 'That we never were members of any Society of the United Irishmen, nor took any oath of Secrecy to that body.'"[9]

Not since the Raising of the Siege had the City gates been closed, but on 25th September 1797 the Mayor and Sheriffs of the City ordered the gates to be shut at nine o'clock each night. This continued up to 1808, when the first of the ancient gates were removed. A point of historical interest is that a single bell (better known as the curfew bell) of St Columb's Cathedral was rung out at nine o'clock every evening from 1797 and this tradition of shutting the ancient gates at nine o'clock still continues right up to the present day. This was a reminder that anyone who lived outside the City had to leave or be locked in overnight. This curfew bell also used to ring out at six-thirty

---

9   Hempton, John. *The Siege and History of Londonderry* (1861) p 335

every morning marking the opening of the City Gates to outside traders. (This was changed to nine o'clock in the morning during the 1960s.)

The Maiden City flourished during the early part of the 19th century and by 1812 the population of the City and its suburbs had increased to 10,000. Of this 1,600 were members of the Church of Ireland, 3,500 were Roman Catholics, and the remainder was made up of dissenters of various religious persuasions. By 1834, the population had grown to 19,000, with Catholics now forming half of the City's population and by 1851 they were in a clear majority. The large migration of Roman Catholics and Nationalists from Donegal settled mainly in the Bogside area, whereas the Protestant community resided mainly in the Fountain suburb of the City. While historical Siege commemorations remained an important part of the cultural calendar for the Protestant community, migration into the City from other parts of Ireland challenged those acts of historical commemorations verbally and by public protest.

Now that the Catholic population was in the majority, there existed some sectarian tensions over the rebellion of 1798 between the two communities. While the Roman Catholic Bishop in the City, Dr O'Donnell, did much to foster and maintain a good working relationship with the predominately Protestant City Corporation and with the City's MP, Sir George Hill, he could not stop the introduction of Daniel O'Connell's national emancipation crusade in the City in 1811. This saw a huge turnout of the Catholic population, with the exception of the local clergy. Dr O'Donnell's political position brought him into conflict with the local Catholic Committee, who denounced him as 'Orange Charlie'. From this point onwards, relationships between certain citizens became frosty; Catholics now had a voice and they would make sure that their voice would be heard.

12th August 1811 saw the first major objection to part of the Relief of Derry Celebration. Seven members of the Londonderry Yeomanry were charged with insubordination for refusing to wear orange lilies in their caps. Ever since the Siege, this was the usual custom from the days of the old Volunteers, and even before this by the citizens of Derry. All seven members were from the Rifle Company and all were Roman Catholics. This happened despite the fact that there were Catholics in some of the other Companies who were quite happy to wear orange lilies to celebrate the day. All seven were dismissed from the Yeomanry after a Court of Inquiry on 13th September 1811. Their main objection to having to wear orange lilies for the Relief of Derry Celebrations was due to the orange lily association with Orangeism. This was obnoxious to Roman Catholics, even though Orangeism had only been established for fourteen years, whereas the lily's connection with the Siege Celebration was more than a century old. It was already agreed that orange lilies were not to be worn on 1st July or on 4th November out of respect for fellow Roman Catholics and Protestants serving in the Yeomanry so as to dismiss party discrimination, which had nothing to do with the Siege Celebrations. As a result of the Court of Inquiry findings, Sir George Hill who commanded the Londonderry Yeomanry forbade the wearing of orange lilies, the accustomed badge of honour among Derry men of all persuasions, out of respect for serving Roman Catholics within their ranks.

On November of the same year, the seven men who were dismissed from the Yeomanry made an appeal to Sir George Hill, acknowledging the justice of the sentence and seeking to be readmitted into the corps. It is likely that they were all reinstated, due to the new position that Sir George Hill took concerning the wearing of orange lilies within the Yeomanry ranks.

An unusual photo of Lundy well and truly alight, taken from the Bogside.

Any hopes that the Catholic Bishop, Dr O'Donnell, had of trying to find a middle ground of reconciliation between Catholic supporters of O'Connell and those who wished to live in peace were soon dashed by one of his own priests, Father Cornelius O'Mullan. This priest was a powerful orator and a staunch supporter of Daniel O'Connell and the Ribbon men. He accused his fellow priests of being 'Orange Papists', and the Derry Corporation of being 'Orange'. Brian Lacy describes what happen next:

> "*The Bishop retaliated by accusing Father O'Mullan of planning his assassination, reported the cleric to the local civil authorities and prohibited him from officiating as a parish priest. On the 28th November of that year, Dr O'Donnell organised a meeting in the Long Tower Church to try and capture control of the Catholic Committee. During the meeting Father O'Mullan, supported by an angry mob which included several Ribbon men, arrived at the Church and physically and verbally threatened the Bishop, who was forced to flee to the courthouse for protection. O'Mullan was immediately ex-communicated by the Bishop and was arrested by the civil authorities.*"[10]

Father Cornelius O'Mullan was tried, convicted and condemned to one month in jail in 1814, followed by a security of peace order for a further two years.

In 1814, the first Apprentice Boys of Derry Club was formed, a precursor of the present-day organisation, and it would be this group who would now emerge as the main driving force behind Derry's two main celebratory days.

---

10 Lacy, Brian. *Siege City* (1990) p 170

First burning of Lundy outside the Courthouse on Saturday 18th December 1974.

As in the 18th century and during the first two decades of the 19th century, the military played a significant part in the 18th Celebrations, but in December 1821 Colonel Pearson (Commander of the Garrison of Londonderry) prevented the military and yeomanry from celebrating the day. *The Londonderry Journal* reports the citizens' astonishment that the Garrison Commander should have issued such orders. It was viewed as:

> "...ill judged, this illegal and unconstitutional order, and which reflects the good temper and spirit of our Yeomanry and Fellow Citizens, and prove them to be not so unworthy of their Gallant Ancestors."

The Yeomanry (400 in total) were only informed on the morning of the 18th Celebration as they formed up to parade.

> "They felt deeply mortified, but with the same sense of discipline which became soldiers and will not permit them to remonstrate, they submitted with respect, but mournful silence, they retired to their respective drill squares and improved themselves in their duty."

Colonel Pearson was not satisfied at just preventing a military presence at the 18th Celebration, he went one step further and issued an order to his piquets to patrol the streets and apprehend anyone caught with or assembling a weapon with the intent of firing it after 8 pm. That night a 14-year-old boy was arrested and dragged through the streets. Sir John Maginnis the Chief Magistrate, the Mayor and other leading figures in the City were not impressed by the Garrison Commander's behaviour and asked the question as to who gave Colonel Pearson such authority to behave in such an unspirited manner.

The young Citizens of the City (totalling 200 plus) took up the cause of the Yeomanry and their gallant defenders, armed themselves, and after forming into three companies, marched to the four gates firing three volleys over each, and then marched to the Diamond. This was followed by three hearty cheers from the crowd before they dispersed. The memory of the Defenders had been honoured despite Colonel Pearson's attempts to dismiss it as but an *"introduction of the house of Brunswick to the British Throne."* The behaviour of Colonel Pearson outraged the community and his behaviour was seen as being no better than that of Colonel Robert Lundy, the garrison commander in 1688. Clear definitions of identity and language representing 'Protestant' and 'Catholic' were beginning to emerge.

A sequel to Pearson's ban was the formation of the No Surrender Apprentice Boys of Derry Club in 1824, whose members joined with the Yeomanry in the Siege commemorations. From 1822 until 1826, the Two Big Days (August and December) were celebrated by the civic authorities supported by the Yeoman Infantry, under the command of Sir G F Hill, Bart.

The laying of the Foundation stone of Walker's monument at the Shutting of the Gates Celebration in 1826 was well received by all. Even the *Londonderry Journal* gave a positive report on the events of the day (Walker's statue was elevated to the top of the Pillar in August 1828). However, by 13th April 1829, tensions were brewing in the City due to the Catholic Emancipation Act, which entitled Catholics to receive the Freedom of the City.

The Catholic community responded to the passing of the Emancipation Act with a parade on St Patrick's Day in 1830, demanding more local political reform. The editor of the *Derry Journal* that December did not help matters by writing an article about the Apprentice Boys and the

Shutting of the Gates Celebration. He regarded the parade as *"a childish and dangerous farce."* The Apprentice Boys of Derry responded through the Londonderry Sentinel by clarifying that the December Celebration,

> *"... is not as the triumph of Civil and Religious Liberty over their Roman Catholic fellow-subjects they observed the day – it is as the triumph of Civil and Religious Liberty over a despicable Tyrant, whose memory all well informed Romanists, detest and in which Civil and Religious Liberty they equally share with Protestants."*

Despite the best efforts of the Catholic Bishop, Dr Peter McLaughlin, in trying to continue the good work of reconciliation between both communities, his frustrations grew through exclusion from the political arena. This led to sporadic disturbances in the early 1830s over the right to hold traditional marches in the City. The Catholic response to the two Protestant traditional parades was to hold one of their own, namely St Patrick's Day, which took place just outside the City walls on 17th March.

Through the Municipal Corporation an enquiry was held to deal with the parades issue. They concluded that,

> *"...parades interrupted industry, alarmed families, widened political differences, embittered religious feuds, provoked collisions of individuals and crowds, produced periodical breaches of the peace and led to the exasperating retaliation and continual disturbance of public tranquillity."*[11]

---

11 Mullin, T H. *Derry Londonderry* (1986) p 141

A HISTORY OF THE SHUTTING OF THE GATES CELEBRATIONS 1775–1985

During the first half of the 19th century various attempts were made by the British Government to ban party parades in Ireland. In 1832 the first Anti-Processions Act became law, making commemoration parades illegal, although a modified format continued in the City for the duration of that Parliament (i.e., five years). On Monday 17th December 1832 the Parliamentary elections took place in the City, where Sir Robert Alexander Ferguson Bart was elected to represent the City in Westminster (a position he held until 1847). The long-standing tradition within the City was that its newly elected member of Parliament should be 'chaired' around the City, lifted up on shoulders of those who carried him. (The original chair was made from the Siege gates and can be found in the Chapter House of the St Columb's Cathedral.) However, due to the fact that the election took place on 17th December, the actual chairing around the City was to be celebrated the following day, 18th December – Lundy's Day. Given the state of excitement among the Citizens at the election results the Mayor, Sir George Hill, thought it advisable to issue a proclamation that no public demonstration should take place in the City to commemorate the Shutting of the Gates, due to the Chairing of the newly elected MP for the City on the same day. The Apprentice Boys had already concluded that no procession would take place, although the dawning of the day had commenced with the beating of the drums and raising the Siege colours on the Cathedral and Walker's Pillar; and it was still expected that Lundy would be hung and burned from the Corporation Hall at the appointed time. The Mayor reacted by ordering that the effigy be removed and held in a secure place, and placed a cordon of police around the Corporation Hall to prevent any further displaying and burning of Lundy. The Apprentice Boys reacted to the Mayor's orders early that afternoon by seizing the stolen effigy from its supposed place of security and taking it to Walker's

Pillar. There it was suspended by a rope from the summit and was then reduced to ashes while the Roaring Meg was fired from the quays. (This was the first time Lundy was burned from the Walker's pillar, and the last time the old 18 pounder, Roaring Meg, was used for salutes.) They then continued to march around the City walls twice, firing their small cannon several times at each of the four Siege gates. This all took place during the period of the 'chairing'. After several prosecutions were made against the Apprentice Boys, they decided to discontinue the use of musketry and music. Later, of course, music was reintroduced and the firing of cannon continued to remain a major part of the Siege Celebrations.

The 'Bottle and Glass' festivities (so called the Bottle and Glass, as each person brought their own bottle of preferred beverage and glass), which formed part of the evening of the 18th Celebrations, was first recorded by *The Londonderry Journal* on 26th December 1815, where it stated that this was a long-standing event. However, it was The *Londonderry Sentinel's* reporting of the Day's Celebrations which captured the mood of the Bottle and Glass event. It stated that:

> "At seven o'clock Corporation Hall was thrown open, and in a short time after one of the most numerous and respectable assemblies ever witnessed on a similar occasion came together, each person with his own 'Bottle and Glass'. The Hall was thronged almost to suffocation, and many of the leading Gentry of the City and neighbourhood were forced to content themselves with room to stand upon their feet. Five hundred, at least, were present. The Chair was taken at eight by that steady and faithful Apprentice Boy, John Murray Esq, Henry Darcus and Marcus Stewart, Esqrs, acted as Croupiers. Shortly after the opening of the meeting, Sir Robert Bateson entered, accompanied by

a number of friends. The Hon Baronet wore a medal and ribbons of the City, and was instantly hailed with the most tremendous applause, which lasted several minutes. After the cheering had subsided he rose up and spoke."

Bateson's address was considerably long, but he did assure his hearers that the spirit of religious freedom and liberty so nobly won by the Apprentices Boys so long ago, was also a cause close to his own heart. The crowd's applause was deafening. This was followed by a list of toasts to the King, the Duke of Cumberland, the Duke of York, the immortal memory of King William the Third, the events of Shutting of the Gates, the health of the Apprentice Boys who that day had stolen the effigy of Lundy from the police, etc. As each toast was made, this was followed by music and hearty singing of *'The Boyne Water', 'No Surrender', 'Protestant Boys', 'Orange and Blue', 'Rule Britannia', 'British Grenadiers'* and *'The Glorious First of August'*. The meeting ended about eleven o'clock, and all left the Hall highly gratified by the evening's events.

The first account of stones being thrown at members of the Apprentice Boys Organisation was in December 1834. It seems there was a group of *'ruffians'* who had made several attempts during the day to cause a riot, but the Mayor and other civic dignitaries, together with the police prevented any major disturbance against those taking part in the Day's Celebrations. This disturbance occurred during the burning of Lundy in King William's Square (the Diamond) late in the afternoon and several Apprentice Boys were injured as they watched the effigy burn. (This was the only occasion where Lundy wore a bottle green coat.) The situation was quickly brought under control by the police and there was no further disturbance that evening.

In 1835 and 1837 the local press reported on the heavy handedness of the City police against those involved in the December Celebrations. In the first instance in December 1835, some enthusiastic Apprentice Boys started to beat their drums before the day started and got into a dispute with the police. This resulted in two house windows being broken in the Bogside and local residents retaliating by throwing missiles at the Apprentice Boys members. It would seem from local reports that this was not the first time that the police took a dim view of the Protestant Celebrations in the City. *The Londonderry Sentinel* reported the event and made reference to the police's behaviour toward the Apprentices, and commented that:

> "We would beg to know why they have not been equally on the alert when the streets were perambulated by thousands of Ribbon men, as, for instance, on the night of January, when a ruffian rabble held the City at their mercy, and on the occasion of Lord Mulgrave's visit to Derry?"

The second incident happened on Derry walls, just after the firing of the first cannon, ushering in the 18th morning (a few minutes before one o clock in the morning). An unusually large body of armed police rushed up onto the walls to the location of the cannon firing led by a Stipendiary Magistrate Captain Roberts of Buncrana. It seemed that a major battle was about to take place between the Apprentices and the police. On their approach several children, who had gathered on the walls to witness the firing of the cannon, fled for safety into the Royal Bastion out of fear of what was going to happen next. No breach of the law was made and all dispersed without incident. This action by the Stipendiary Magistrate and the police resolutely embedded a Siege mentality: that the traditional Siege Celebrations of 1688-89 were not to be interfered with.

1837 and 1838 witnessed the doors of the Cathedral closed to the vast crowd gathered in the City from Donegal and Tyrone for the 18th Celebration. The Crimson flag was hoisted as usual and the Cathedral bells rung all day, but Walker's pulpit was silent, much to the disgust of the Apprentice Boys Association. There is one possible reason why this happened. In 1836 the introduction of the Anti-Procession Act would have brought the Church and State into conflict with each other. The Church of Ireland at the time was the state church in Ireland and therefore it was important that it should been seen to lead the way in upholding the Laws of the Land. Mr George Hill Esq alludes to this very fact in his toast to the Lord Primate and the Church of Ireland in 1838, by stating, *'that he was the head of a family, who have been distinguished for their identity to the cause of Protestantism,'* but due to the political pressures placed on him, he was doing what he thought best.

Disagreement between Catholics citizens about the Shutting of the Gates festivities also occurred in 1837, resulting in a complete withdrawal from it, much to the disappointment of the Protestant community.

The first occasion in which cannon was not used for ushering in the 18th morning was in 1840. The principal reason for the Apprentice Boys making this decision was due to one of the cannons exploding on the walls on 12th August, killing a Mr Thomas Fleming, injuring Mr John Platt (who lost his eyesight), and wounding Mr Robert Orr. But by 1841 the cannons were in full use again.

1842 saw the second burning of the Lundy effigy from Walker's Pillar from a beam which projected out from the roof of the east end of the Corporation Hall in the Diamond, rather than from its usual place of incineration. This long-standing tradition was to continue until Walker's Pillar was destroyed by a 100lb bomb in 1973.

The first objection from the Catholic community to the 18th Celebration, took place on the evening of 18th December 1843 in the City Council Chamber, where Alderman Mehan and Mr Casey, speaking on behalf of the Catholic Community said that this burning of Lundy was *an insult to themselves and their creed.* Two other liberal Protestant members, Mr John Leathem and Doctor Rogan, were of the opinion that the Mayor should have exercised his legal powers and prevented the burning of the effigy, as no Mayoral consent had been granted for this burning to take place.

In ensuing years, the 18th Celebrations continued without any disturbance and some Catholics mixed with the crowd who annually gathered to witness and enjoy the mock burning of the Siege traitor.

On the occasion of the 161st Anniversary of the Shutting of the Gates (1850), a rumour circulated that effigies of Cardinal Wiseman and the Pope were to be burned alongside Lundy on the 18th. The new Catholic Bishop, Dr Francis Kelly had done much work in the City to restore a spirit of goodwill. This had been damaged by his predecessor, Dr Edward Maginn, who was a strong supporter of Daniel O'Connell and who campaigned against Protestant parades in the City. Bishop Kelly raised his concerns with the Chief Magistrate and Sir Robert Ferguson MP, they in turn informed the Mayor of the City (Mr Murray) and he called a meeting of the local magistrates to discuss a plan of action. Several political preventive measures were implemented. The first was that notices would be placed around the City that any attempt to burn any other effigies other than Lundy would be a breach of the Anti-Procession Act, resulting in a fine of up to 10 shillings for burning an effigy in any public place. To save political face, this notice did not contain a single signature making it official. It was even rumoured that it was the local Tenant League that was responsible for its posting it around the City. There was also political division over effigy burning, including that of Lundy, between those who had gathered in the Apprentice Boys meeting. Lundy had at long last found friends in Mr Haslett, Mr Mehan and Mr Coulson, who strongly objected to the Apprentice Boys cause, whereas, the Mayor, Mr Murray and Mr Dysart opposed any inference of the magistrates with this part of the Celebrations, although all were in agreement in thinking that a procession with field-pieces was illegal. They believed that to interfere with the burning of Lundy would result in several possible burning of Lundy effigies in various parts of the City, which would have caused more problems for the authorities. As a preventive measure and again to save political face, it was agreed that a police force of 100 men would be drafted into the City and that an RM (Resident Magistrate) from Omagh, a Captain Coulson would deal with any breaches of the Law at the 18th Celebrations.

At twelve midnight on the eve of the 18th, a salvo of artillery was fired on the City ramparts and cheers were given in honour of the day by the large crowd of Apprentices and citizens who had gathered to witness the event. Under Head Constable Magee, no opposition was offered by the authorities. Names were taken by his officers, but no arrests were made and the cannons were not confiscated. Just before nine o'clock on the 18th morning, the Apprentice Boys were again discharging cannon fire on the same spot. At this the Mayor and Captain Coulson made their appearance on the walls, the latter read the riot act to the young Apprentices and assured them that a large body of police were on their way to their location. At this the young Apprentices ceased firing and placed their cannon in the Irish Society's Bastion and where they were guarded by police with muskets throughout the day and well into the night. The remainder of the day was celebrated in usual style and Lundy was the only effigy burned from Walker's Pillar. But all was not quiet, as several ruffians from the Bogside area made their way up into the centre of the City and attacked several Protestants returning to their homes from the evening Celebrations. It was also reported that there was another an effigy of an unknown Lundy burned in the Bogside that evening, but that no arrests were made.

1851 saw the introduction of the crimson sash as a means of parade dress for the Apprentice Boys Association. Up to this point only crimson ribbon was worn on the lapel. By 1844, Mr James William Gregg Esq, President of the Apprentice Boys of Derry Club wore an elegant star of office. By 1845, he is described as wearing his star as a badge of his office and carrying his mallet of the freedom of the City, as he led the procession to the Cathedral for the Divine Service. Other Presidents of other Clubs followed suit in wearing their respective badge of office, and leading their own Clubs in the procession to the Cathedral for the Celebration service. On the 18th December 1848, all who were members of the Apprentice Boys Association wore crimson ribbons attached to medals impressed with the Reverend George Walker on one side and on the reverse side, the Relief of Derry. As before, all of the Club Presidents wore their respective star badge of office.

One of the most significant attempts to stop the Apprentice Boys Celebrations was in 1860, with the introduction of the Party Emblems Act. The was to make the Anti-Processions Act more stringent, as the latter did not apply to the Derry Celebrations. This new Party Emblems Act consisted of the following five pieces of legislation in relation to:

1. The publicly exhibiting of displaying upon any building or place, any banner, flag, party emblem or symbol.
2. The wilfully permitting or suffering to be publicly exhibited, or displayed upon building or place, any banner, flag, party emblem or symbol.
3. The public meeting, and parading, with other persons in any public street, road or place.
4. Playing any music, in a public street, road or place.
5. Discharging any cannon or firearms in any public street, road or place.

This Act was to be enforced over the next five years, and the Apprentice Boys organisation were yet again having to stand firm, explain, and expose those who were determined to put an end to their longstanding customary Celebrations.

The person responsible for raising this Act in Dublin and in the House of Commons was Mr Acheson Lyle, Lieutenant for the County of Londonderry and Chief Justice of the Peace. He opposed the Apprentice Boys Celebrations and he certainly used both his local knowledge and his political friends in both Dublin Castle and in the Houses of Parliament to champion his cause. It was debated in both places that the Apprentice Boys of Derry Organisation was but another branch of the lawless Orange Order and that there was an ever-present danger of Ribbon men from Donegal attacking one of these parades, thus putting lives in danger. In fact, Mr Lyle did his very best to try to persuade the Reverend Beresford to swear that the hoisting of the Crimson flag on the ancient Cathedral would lead to a breach of the peace. The Apprentice Boys Organisation also had their own champions to dispel such false accusations: Mr Vance, member for Dublin, and Lord Claude Hamilton, one of the representatives for Tyrone. It was argued that the Derry Celebrations had nothing to do with the Orange Order and that the Celebrations existed long before the present celebration of the Battle of the Boyne. Furthermore, there was no real opposition to the Party Emblems Act, if it be carried out impartially. The reporter of the *Londonderry Sentinel* highlighted the strong concerns that the people felt about this new piece of legislation which was being forced upon them. He wrote that:

> *"The spirit of it is right, so far as regards the non-provocation of animosity and the promotion of peace, for in these respects it coincides with the common law, but the details are vague and leaves the best disposed men at the mercy of hard swearing and tyrannical arbitrary interpretation."*

On the basis of this, it was argued that no fair construction could make the Party Emblems Act apply to the Derry Celebrations as it was a civic occasion, and that the majority of both religious communities enjoyed the Siege festivities. These events were not an act of Protestant triumphalism, but an act of religious and political freedom, about deliverance from an oppressive tyrannical power.

The 18th Celebrations of 1860, saw a very large crowd of people pour into the City (this was largely due to the rail network). The Apprentice Boys were anxious to adhere to this new Law and consulted the best English and Irish counsel, who were unanimous in their opinion that this Act could not apply to them as the Celebration was a civic demonstration.

The response of the authorities in Dublin Castle and Parliament was to send 300 men of the 86th Regiment under the command of Colonel

Stewart, two troops of the 3rd Dragoons, under Captain Diamond, and 300 constabulary, under the direction of Colonel Wood. Deputy Inspector General R D Coulson Esq, RM, from Omagh, and Charles Hunt, RM, from Ballymena took charge over local magistracy, carrying out the orders of government. After much discussion the Apprentice Boys decided to comply with the Law and not fire the cannon in the morning part of the Celebrations but to wait until the afternoon. Not all were happy about the decision made by the General Committee of the Association. The Mitchelburne Club, whose cannons were stored elsewhere, and not at Mr James Gregg Esq, of Pump Street, decided not to break the law, but rather to test the Act as to whether or not it did have a bearing on the Siege Celebration. They brought out one of their field pieces and passed through London Street, to Bishop Street, to the Mall Wall, where a position was taken up and six shots were fired, amidst loud cheers from the crowd who had gathered on the walls. Some of the Apprentice Boys who witnessed this action were displeased that the Mitchelburne Club had gone against the wishes of the General Committee. Mr Coulson RM hastened to the spot and asked the gunners not to break the law and took their names, but he made no attempt to confiscate the cannon. The remainder of the day passed off peacefully and the Apprentice Boys felt vindicated as the Siege Celebration in the City was seen as neither political, nor an insult to those of the Catholic community.

A new addition to the burning of Lundy in 1862 was the formation of the Apprentice Boys band, called the Maiden City, who took up their place at the North-West Bastion and played during the firing of the cannon and burning of the Lundy effigy. Their standard of music was described as having improved from previous events. This year also witnessed a division between the classes who celebrated the day's events.

At six o'clock in the evening, about forty gentlemen connected with the professional and commercial interests in the City sat down to an excellent dinner in McCormick's hotel, Foyle Terrace, to commemorate the Closing of the Gates in 1688. This festive dinner was to revive a custom which was carried out by Derry men in memory of the gallant defenders of Derry's Siege. Among the many toasts offered by these gentlemen, there was one offered to the Apprentice Boys who were still celebrating the events of the day outside in the streets and in the Corporation Hall. By 1864 it was the Apprentice Boys Association which had taken on the responsibility for organising the Commemoration Dinner. The location was at the Imperial Hotel, and again it was now a select number of elite Apprentice Boys and citizens of various classes who attended, while the Mitchelburne, Campsie and Browning Clubs dined together in the large Pianoforte Show Room connected with Mr John Hempton's music warehouse, which was situated in the Diamond. These annual commemoration dinners continued to 1881, but became more sporadic toward the end of the 1800s. Evening Soirees continued in the Corporation Hall, and in 1877 the Inauguration Ball was introduced, following on from the Soiree. This was the last year that the Apprentice Boys would use this venue, due to the building of the new Apprentice Boys of Derry Memorial Hall in Society Street.

The City remained quiet for the next few years, but on 28th April 1869 trouble erupted between some of the Apprentice Boys and Catholics from the Bogside, resulting in the death of two people, Mr William Craig, a rope spinner, aged 20, and Mr Robert Moncrieff, a mechanic, aged 18. One was a Church of Ireland member and the other was a Presbyterian. A third man Mr William Murphy of the Creggan, died from a gunshot wound in June 1869. The Jury's inquest found that in Moncrieff's case he was shot by the police, whereas an open verdict was returned for Craig. This was the result of an overnight visit to the City by Prince Arthur (one of Queen Victoria's sons). There was much excitement and tension in equal measure in the City on this occasion. The Prince was staying in the Imperial Hotel and at approximately 8 pm a large crowd of Protestants emerged from Bishop Street, and as the two rival groups met, they started to hurl stones and insults at each other in the Diamond area. As the situation became more aggressive, the police (who were in the middle) had no alternative but to step in between the two factions with fixed bayonets. During this time two shots were fired by the mob, and the police had no other choice but to return the fire and did their level best to restore order in the City centre. The crowd from the Bogside were eventually pushed down Butcher Street, but would go no further. Their spokesman Mr Stafford said that his people feared the crowd of Protestants, who by this time had made their way up onto Derry walls, overlooking the Butcher Gate section of the walls. The concern was that this crowd would start to shoot down at them, as well as stone them. At this point, the police mounted the walls over the Gateway and started to push the Protestants up toward Walker's Pillar, aided by the Governor of the Apprentice Boys Association, Mr John Guy Ferguson. The intervention of both men succeeded in helping to restore peace in the City that night. This incident led to a call from the City's Liberal Party for a ban on all parades, but their appeal was ignored.

The Apprentice Boys Association at this time had a membership of 300 ordinary members, i.e. those who lived in the City, and 200 honorary members, such as William Johnston, MP for Belfast. The total of Clubs in existence in 1869 were the following seven: The Apprentice Boys of Derry Club, the Walker Club, The Murray Club, The Mitchelburne Club, the Williamite Club, The Baker and The No Surrender Clubs.

The events of April 1869 saw the formation of the Liberal Working Men's Association, under the leadership of a publican from William Street, Mr John O'Donnell. They were supported by the local Liberal leaders (many of them were Presbyterians), who were opposed to the more Catholic radical element, but were not afraid to voice their support for this new movement in the City. The position of the Liberal Working Men's Association was clear, in that they were determined to put an end to the Celebrations, even if it meant using force. They claimed that they had the support of a vast number of their friends from the surrounding area that they could call upon to assist them in their cause.

There was much tension in the City with the approaching 18th December Celebrations. On Friday 17th December the Governor of the Apprentice Boys (John Guy Ferguson) called a meeting in the Pump Street Schoolroom. A vast crowd gathered and various guest speakers addressed them, including William Johnston MP, Mr John Madden JP, Captain Charles Madden and Mr Hunt Chambers. Among the many speeches uttered that evening, wise counsel was offered by the Governor of the Association to uphold the decision made by the Local Resident Magistrates for the closure of all public houses in the City on the Saturday from seven o'clock in the morning of the 18th to two o'clock in the afternoon of Sunday the 19th. This curfew was not strictly adhered to as several men were seen staggering around on the 18th in the City centre. With the 1869 Peace Preservation Act in place, the Apprentice Boys removed their cannon from their present location to another county to prevent the authorities from confiscating them.

When the 181st anniversary of the Shutting of the Gates arrived, it was rumoured that a large crowd of men armed with clubs, sticks and guns from the Bogside and contingents from Inishowen, were making their way up outer Bishop Street. Their purpose was to prevent the Apprentices Boys from marching up Bishop Street from the Corporation Hall to the Cathedral for their Divine Service. Security was tight as the authorities expected a riot in the area of Bishop Street. To ensure that this would not happen, 1,500 military troops were drafted into the City to support and assist the Royal Irish Constabulary. Four companies of the 17th Regiment had been quartered at the Court House under Colonel Cobb. Colonel Brown of the 44th Regiment, which consisted of seven companies, was quartered at the Potato Market in Society Street and a further squadron of the 8th Hussars, under Captain Le Mallet, were stationed in Sir Edward Reid's Market. The number of Constabulary in the City was 750 men, under the command of John Reid, who was Deputy Inspector-General. The resident Magistrates sent into the City on this occasion were J C O'Donnell RM, Captain Keogh, Mr Joseph Eglington Esq, and Mr J Goold Esq.

The 18th morning was ushered in at 6.30 am with the hoisting of the Siege flags on the Cathedral, Walker's Pillar, the Corporation Hall and the bastions on the City walls. Simultaneously, the effigy of Lundy, which had been lying across the top of the Pillar since Thursday night, was suspended by a rope from the top and kept dangling near the top all day. The whole morning's proceedings were carried out to the sound of the Cathedral joy bells ringing.

Shortly after ten o'clock the Apprentice Boys gathered for a public meeting in the Corporation Hall, which was filled to its extremity. Meanwhile, the Britannia Flute Band marched from their band room in Magazine Street toward the Corporation Hall, where they were greeted with loud cheers from the crowd that had gathered both inside and outside the Hall. Having made all the necessary preparations inside the Hall for the procession to the Cathedral, the Governor of the Apprentice Boys (John Guy Ferguson) addressed the crowd, repeating the advice he had given to them on the previous evening. Firstly, that they were resolved to carry out their intended programme in a manner that would not jeopardise any future Celebrations. Secondly, that no retaliation would be made to any attacks to the parade. Lastly, that by conducting themselves in a dignified manner, the Government would protect their Association and traditions. Speeches concluded, the parade formed up outside the Corporation Hall and were led by bands marched up Bishop Street to the tune of 'No Surrender'. They were accompanied by a cordon of police on either side and men of the 17th Regiment, who with fixed bayonets, formed into a column and marched up behind the procession to the Court House. The remainder of the parade made its way via Society Street to the City walls and there re-formed. The main procession, whose members generally wore crimson sashes and rosettes, led by the Governor of the Association, made its way down Magazine Street, up Shipquay Street to Bishop Street, into St Columb's Court and up the steps into the Cathedral, where they were again met by a large crowd.

On leaving the Cathedral, the Apprentice Boys re-formed in procession order in St Columb's Court and marched down Bishop Street, around the Diamond, back up Bishop Street and down Society Street to Walker's Pillar. Moving South, the parade did a circuit of the walls, marched across Society Street and London Street to Pump Street, down Pump Street and Ferryquay Gate, countermarched to Butcher Gate, Shipquay Gate, Bishop Gate, and lastly paraded to the Royal Bastion for the burning of Lundy. Along the entire route the Apprentice Boys Association was greeted by cheers from the crowd that had especially gathered in the City for the 18th Celebrations. The crowd was dense on the walls from Butcher Gate right up to the Royal Bastion, spilling into Society Street, all eager to get a good view of the Lundy effigy burning from Walker's Pillar. At three o'clock, the effigy of Lundy was being slowly lowered from the top of the Pillar, but due to the heavy rain (making the effigy heavier than usual), the rope broke when he was halfway down and Lundy fell to the ground, knocking off the hat of one of the men who was standing on the top of the square base, waiting to ignite him. The rope was fixed, but as soon as they began to raise the effigy, it broke a second time, giving Lundy a second fall. A new rope was then obtained and after a little delay, Lundy was on fire. He burned very slowly and by this time many of those who had gathered in great anticipation to witness the burning left the City walls, having been drenched in the rain. They had departed before his legs were consumed with fire.

The only incident throughout the whole day happened during the burning of Lundy by one or possibly two over enthusiastic persons. Unknown to the Dean and local authorities, several cannon shots were heard from the top of the Cathedral roof. The authorities made their way up onto the roof of the Cathedral and seized the small cannon, but not the person or persons who were responsible for firing it.

Later that evening there was the usual Commemoration Dinner at the Imperial Hotel and a supper in the Corporation Hall, but the usual Soiree and Ball was postponed to the Monday night, so as to maintain the Sabbath Day. Despite the threats from the Catholics and the Working Men's Liberal Association, no attempt was made to stop the Celebrations from taking place; instead they were content to burn effigies of Cromwell and Lord Castlereagh (an Orange Order champion) in the Bogside.

1870 was the most contentious year for the Apprentice Boys Association. The Liberal Working Men's Defence Association issued a manifesto prior to the Relief of Derry Celebrations in August, calling on the Catholics of Ulster to assemble in the Maiden City to put an end to the insults inflicted on them by this Protestant Association. On 3rd December, John O'Donnell, President of the Defence Association published a letter in the local newspaper that the Society, saying it:

> "Cannot and will not be dissolved until its members shall have received full and perfect assurance that all insulting displays which hitherto have disgraced this City shall be abolished."

The Lord Lieutenant condemned the Defence Association and was surprised that no steps had been taken to punish its ringleaders. The Government's response was that the Defence Association posed no threat; in fact, they helped to support them. While it seemed that the objectives of John O'Donnell had failed in a total outright ban of the 18th Celebrations at a Governmental level, his case was taken up by Captain Keogh RM, and seven liberal magistrates issued a proclamation on the 9th declaring that all processions in the City were to be banned. They knew that to enforce such a Ban would require a large force to implement it and so extensive preparations were made to ensure that peace would be preserved within the City and that the Ban would be upheld. On Thursday 15th December, 1,000 extra Royal Irish Constabulary were drafted into the City to help boost policing in the City over the next few days. They were drafted in from Donegal, Tyrone, Fermanagh, Leitrim, Cavan, Antrim, Down Sligo, Louth and Monaghan. Each Constabulary had its own Sub-Inspector. To support the Constabulary, two companies of the 80th (Staffordshire Volunteers) Regiment from Armagh, under the command of Captain Crawford, Lieutenant Swinburne and Ensign Power, arrived by train on

Saturday 17th December. A further 200 soldiers from the same cap-badge, under the command of Captain Ariel, arrived from Belfast later in the day. At half-past five on the same day, the 6th Dragoon Guards arrived from Dundalk and were commanded by Lieutenant Rippingdale. They were soon followed by the 16th Regiment from their Headquarters in Newry, commanded by Captain Alcock. A contingent from the 16th Regiment was already stationed in Ebrington Barracks along with the City's contingent of Constabulary. The overall military commander of this operation was Lieutenant Colonel George E Hillier, Deputy Inspector-General of the Royal Irish Constabulary, assisted by the Country Inspector, Fanning. Henry Keogh Esq was the overall magistrate in charge.

The logistical task of where to billet such a large force was no mean feat. Some of men for the 80th Regiment were quartered in the military barracks and the remainder of the military, along with the 6th Dragoon Guards, were billeted in the various barracks in and around the City. The majority of the Constabulary was accommodated in Straw Lodges. New housing erected by Mr Johnstone at Ferryquay Gate was full, as were premises belonging to Mr Evans in Pump Street and Mr Greer in the same street, together with the properties of Mr Hughes of Waterloo Street, and the commercial offices of Mr Bigger in Foyle Street. Others were based in the Barracks in Shipquay Street and in Sackville Street.

On Thursday 15th, a guard of Constabulary was placed around Walker's Pillar and all along the ramparts of the walls. Half of the men on this duty had their swords, and by the afternoon all civilians were denied access on to the walls. By midday the role of the Constabulary was to be tested by a civilian who demanded access to walk along the walls, declaring that it was his right to do so. The civilian was directed to take up his case with Lieutenant Colonel Hillier, but needless to say nothing materialised.

Throughout Thursday night, Friday morning and all day Saturday, the police searched for the Lundy effigy which had mysteriously disappeared on Saturday morning from the Apprentice Boys Memorial Hall in Society Street. During the entire Saturday 17th there was great excitement and much joking as to Lundy's whereabouts, which was embarrassing for the Constabulary as they continued to search key locations in the City. Lieutenant Colonel Hillier applied for permission to have the Bishop's Palace, its grounds and the Cathedral searched, hoping to find Lundy there. Eleanor Alexander takes up the story of the Constabulary's arrival at the Bishop's Palace.

> *"The police arrived at the Palace with a search-warrant. Mrs Alexander, who was at home, met them in the hall. 'Have you a stuffed figure in the house?' asked the rather shamed-faced officer. 'Yes,' said Mrs Alexander. 'Several. My little girls play with dolls.'"* [12]

Bishop Alexander arrived at the Palace as the Constabulary were about to leave. They demanded the keys for the Cathedral, but were refused on the basis that he would not permit anything illegal to take place in the Cathedral.

Just after six o'clock on Saturday evening a placard was posted in all of the leading thoroughfares, stating that:

> *"The Apprentice Boys beg to inform the citizens of Derry that the burning of Lundy is postponed for the present. The illegal and unconstitutional action of the partisan magistrates of Derry backed by*

---

12   Alexander, Eleanor. *Primate Alexander Archbishop of Armagh* (1913) p 162

an overwhelming military and police force supplied by our benevolent Government, renders the above necessary.
By Order, Thomas Mooney Secretary."

That Saturday evening a meeting of the Apprentice Boys was held in the Pump Street School House, which was completely packed. John Guy Ferguson, Governor of the Association took the chair. His address was brief, but resolute, providing clear guidance as to how their members should behave and that they should not get embroiled or feel intimidated by such a large force in the City. He assured them that the Apprentice Boys Association would maintain every part of their accustomed Celebrations no matter what. At the conclusion of the meeting an elected deputation led by Brother John Guy Ferguson, and which included Mr Colhound, Mr Vickers TC, Mr A M Corkell TC, Mr Benjamin Darcus, Mr George Ferguson, and Mr William Hanna, made their way to the Royal Bastion at ten o'clock to hoist the Crimson flag at the top of Walker's Pillar on the eve of the 18th Celebrations. They ascended the walls by the steps at Magazine Street near the Chapel of Ease and made their way to the entrance of Walker's Bastion. The object of their visit was made clear to Captain Coote RM, and Mr O'Donnell RM, along with Sub-Inspector Lawler, the former RM who introduced them to Colonel Hillier. A strong police presence was mounted in the Bastion, they had bayonets fixed, awaiting their orders. John Guy Ferguson entered into dialogue with Colonel Hillier, stating that he was Governor of the Apprentice Boys Association and as Walker's Pillar was raised by public subscription, he like any other member of the public had free access to it at any time, particularly at civic anniversaries. Colonel Hillier stated that *"the magistrates had given this point careful consideration and their decision was that admittance should not be allowed, and he was prepared to resist any attempt to enter the bastion."* Mr Guy Ferguson attempted to push his way through the gate to the bastion, but was pushed back by a constable. That Saturday evening the streets of the City remained quiet, until midnight when the 18th Celebration was ushered in by the firing of two shots from a very small gun. This was the first time a small cannon had been used to usher in the Big Days, and much to the force's annoyance it was a clear violation of the Law.

As the 18th Celebration fell on the Sabbath Day, it was decided that the usual parade to the Cathedral would be observed and that all other 18th activities would happen on the Monday. At half past nine the Cathedral hosted the Crimson flag over the chancel to the sound of the accustomed Cathedral joy bells. This was the first occasion that no crimson flag flew at the top of Walker's Pillar since it was built in 1828.

The streets were a hive of activity, as both well-wishers and objectors gathered at principal rallying points in the City. The Constabulary did their best to try and prevent large groups from gathering in these key areas, but the crowds were overwhelming. Colonel Hiller, the Mayor and the resident Magistrate were all in attendance observing and assessing the growing tension in the vicinity of the Butcher and Bishop Street area.

Shortly after eleven o'clock one of the bands belonging to the Apprentice Boys emerged from their band room in Stable Lane into Bishop Street and made their way to the Corporation Hall to meet up with the rest of the procession. They wore band uniforms with crimson rosettes on their lapels, but carried no instruments. As they approached the Corporation Hall they were greeted with loud hissing and groans from a crowd who had come up from the Bogside and into Butcher Street side of the Hall. The Constabulary dispersed the hissing crowd at Butcher Street.

The Apprentice Boys had been gathering at the Corporation Hall in the Diamond from around eleven o'clock, where they put on their crimson sashes and waited for the appointed time for the procession to form up outside the Hall. At twenty to twelve the parade formed up, headed by the Governor of the Association Mr Guy Ferguson and Lord Garvagh. At three abreast, with no flags or music the whole parade marched around the Hall, up Bishop Street, into St Columb's Court and up the steps into a thronged Cathedral for the Divine Service, led by the Britannia Flute Band. As the Apprentice Boys paraded to the Cathedral, one of the last Apprentices in the procession had his sash torn off in Bishop Street by a Mr O'Neill from Wapping, who made off with it into a sympathetic crowd. The Constabulary did nothing about the incident. A further incident happened at St Columb's Court, where a girl snatched a crimson sash from one of the young men. She waved it triumphantly amid cheers from the nationalists, before she made off with it. At this the Constabulary moved in and cleared the mob away. As the parade processed from the Corporation Hall to the Cathedral, amid all the loud hissing and groaning there was derogatory shouting from the nationalists: "Where's Lundy?" "Have you burned Lundy?" The Apprentice Boys did not react and conducted themselves in a dignified and peaceful manner.

On leaving the Cathedral the Apprentice Boys, led by the Governor paraded down Bishop Street into the Diamond, but instead of entering the Corporation Hall, they proceeded to march down Shipquay Street towards Shipquay Gate. Having reached the Gate, stones were thrown down at them from a crowd who had gathered there. Some of the Apprentice Boys made an attempt to get onto the wall but were pushed backed by the police. Colonel Hillier, who was at hand, gave the order for the crowd to be removed from the walls. One of his officers was thrown from his horse and sustained serious injuries. The Apprentice Boys returned to the Corporation Hall and dispersed. The City remained quiet for the remainder of the day until two o'clock, when a number of people from the Bogside armed with sticks marched through the street inside the walls and through the Wapping. The rest of the day passed off peacefully. The police, however, maintained a strong presence on the walls, especially around the Walker's Bastion.

As dawn broke that Monday morning, some discharges were heard in the City. It was said that these discharges resembling small ordnance were nothing more than some oil cans charged with gunpowder, exploding in some people's backyards. By six o'clock the army and people were in position and prepared for all eventualities. At eleven o'clock the Crimson flag was hoisted on top of the Corporation Hall and there was great excitement in the streets. Many of the shopkeepers shut their shops, anticipating trouble. The police demonstrated a strong presence at the front of the Band Room of the Apprentice Boys at the corner of Society Street and Magazine Street. The band had been practising all morning and by now had attracted a large crowd. The bandsmen seeing the large police presence outside their Band Room, filtered out one by one, each man carrying his own instrument, they made their way to the Corporation Hall and entered in.

All access to the City walls was blocked by the police with rifles and fixed bayonets. The Apprentice Boys had been gathering at the Corporation Hall all morning, but owing to the Government restrictions were forced to remain inside the Hall. At two o'clock the Governor of the Apprentice Boys, Mr Ferguson, appeared at the front door of the Corporation Hall with a large Crimson flag and applied to Colonel Hillier, Captain Coats RM, and J C O'Donnell RM, for leave to have their procession. The application was refused. An attempt was made by them to force their way out onto the street, but they were pushed back and almost lost their Crimson flag in the whole process. Colonel Hillier read out The Party Procession Act and assured them that he would use extreme force if they tried to break the Law. The Colonel further proceeded to warn them that if a single Crimson flag was flown out of any of the windows of the Hall, he would send in the police and remove it by force. Also, that if the Maiden City or the Britannia Bands played any other airs other than what had been submitted to the police, then Colonel Hillier would give the order for the police with fixed bayonets to move in and disperse all of those gathered in the Hall.

Lord Claud John Hamilton MP and Mr John Rea (a solicitor from Belfast) joined the Governor of the Apprentice Boys in the Corporation Hall offering support and solidarity. A meeting of the Apprentice Boys took place where rousing speeches were made by the Governor Mr Ferguson, Mr Rea and others. At the conclusion of the meeting when the Maiden City or the Britannia Bands played various Protestant airs, there was sudden excitement when the window was opened leading out onto a small platform facing Shipquay. A cry was heard to 'barricade the doors', which gave birth to suspicions that an effigy of Lundy was about to make an appearance, which it did, being suspended from the roof of the Hall. It would seem that materials for the effigy had been smuggled into the hall inside the shells of the band drums, where he was hastily put together and duly suspended by a rope from the Corporation Hall roof facing Shipquay Street. The reaction from the large crowds gathered in the Diamond, Shipquay and Ferryquay Street area was twofold. There were those who cheered, and others responded by hissing and jeering. As soon as the effigy of Lundy appeared, he was lowered and set alight. The flame soon burned through the rope and Lundy's feet partly burned, landing on the railings around the Corporation Hall.

The military sprang into action clearing the crowds in the Diamond area with fixed bayonets, while two bodies of police also with fixed bayonets forced their way into the Hall. The Hall was densely populated and each policeman pointed his bayonet at the chests of those who could not move away. The Maiden City Band who occupied the Gallery in the Hall, passed their drums down to the crowd in the main Hall to avoid the police from capturing them. Flags and other insignia were also passed down and placed under the platform for safe keeping. Colonel Hillier and Mr T W D Humphreys JP (the latter was welcomed by the Apprentices in the Hall, with loud cheers), were soon joined by the Mayor, who ordered the withdrawal of the troops. Injuries to those in the Hall were minimal. The Governor of the Apprentices along with Mr Rea and Mr Humphreys took their seats on the platform along with several other speakers. When the meeting concluded, all three men were lifted in their chairs and carried down by the crowd in the Hall to the front doors. On their arrival at the blocked doors, Mr Rea appealed in vain to the Constabulary who had placed a double cordon of police with fixed bayonets around each doorway of the Hall, not even allowing members of the press to leave. Mr Rea continued to protest against the action of the police, resulting in his arrest for obstructing Colonel Hillier in his duty. Several others were also arrested, including Mr Ferguson, the Governor, a young man named McNeely from Bishop Street, and Mr Heaney, a shoe maker. The Hall assembly were then permitted to leave and searched as they left. Once the Hall had been cleared, the police made a thorough search of the place for arms, but none were found.

Mr Rea, Mr McNeely and Mr Heaney were brought before his Worship the Mayor at a special hearing in the Crown Court around six o'clock in the evening. The Governor, Mr Ferguson, must have been released shortly after his arrest as he was not standing with them in the dock. The custody Constable, Mr James Neill, in reply to his Worship, said that he had no warrant for holding the prisoners in custody. He had no orders given to him, except that Sub-Inspector Joyce ordered them to be arrested. Mr Rea said after the Constable's statement that if he was not aware of any charges against him then he would bring a civil case against Colonel Hillier for a common assault. At this, the Mayor sent a written message to Colonel Hillier, stating that he was sitting in an open court and required his attendance. Both Mr McNeely and Mr Heaney also objected to their arrest without charge and demanded their release. Several other witnesses were permitted into the Court hearing, including the Governor, Mr Ferguson. Not long after this Colonel Hillier and Mr John Charles O'Donnell RM arrived at the Court, Colonel Hillier taking his seat on the bench beside the Mayor, O'Donnell standing behind him. The Mayor asked Colonel Hillier what his charge was against Mr Rea. He replied that he had not written it up as yet, but would do so soon as he could, and furthermore he had no objection to Mr Rea being bailed. Mr Rea strongly objected to the whisperings between Colonel Hillier and Mr O'Donnell, stating that the Colonel was able to speak for himself. Mr Rea then appealed to the Mayor for the Colonel to take the witness box and be cross-examined. The Mayor again said to the Colonel that unless he stated the charge, he would discharge him. Colonel Hillier replied, *"I arrested these gentlemen in the discharge of my duty, at a very exciting moment. I will be able to sustain a charge against them."* Once again, the Mayor asked what were the charges against the men. Hillier gave the same reply. At this the

Mayor discharged all three prisoners. Colonel Hillier shook the Mayor's hand and retired, then the Court rose.

The Streets of the City were crowded that evening, but there were no further disturbances and by eleven o'clock all was quiet. The Bogside gentry were disappointed that the Apprentice Boys managed to burn their Lundy despite the large police and military presence in the Diamond area. Just after half past six approximately fifty gentry sat down for the annual Anniversary Banquet in the Imperial Hotel in Bishop Street. On their release from Court, Mr Rea and the Governor of the Association joined them for dinner, where they received a rapturous applause as they entered the room.

Retrospectively, the Apprentice Boys Association was quite pleased with the events of the past few turbulent days. They fired their cannon, flags were raised, the Divine Service took place, they played their music and Lundy was still burned, maintaining a long-standing tradition. The spirit of the brave Thirteen Apprentice Boys was displayed yet again with great success.

With the approaching 18th December Celebrations in 1871, the Apprentice Boys Association did not issue its usual programme. Instead they posted a placard on the walls in the early hours of Thursday 14th. It read:

"Anniversary of the Shutting of the Gates 7th December, O.S., 1688 – Burning of Lundy – The Apprentice Boys beg to inform the citizens that this being the anniversary of the shutting of the gates – 7th December -1688 – the effigy of the traitor Lundy will be burned on Walker's Pillar at three o'clock pm. The course now taken being unusual, it is necessary to state that the unconstitutional conduct of the Irish

Executive in placing the available military and police force in Ireland at the disposal of a few incapable stipendiary magistrates, to crush us by brute force, brought us to the conclusion that this arrangement was advisable. We are also prompted by a feeling of humanity towards the constabulary force, as it was most fearful to see hundreds of splendid-looking men kept exposed by their out-manoeuvred commanders to all rigour of a most severe Northern Winter, for no object but to cover their great failure. The other portions of our Celebration proceedings will take place as usual on the 18th inst. – By order, Thomas Mooney, secretary."

No sooner had this notice been posted, it was torn down by an unknown person. Thomas Mooney issued a notice of a one-pound sterling reward for the name of the perpetrator; needless to say, he did not have to pay up! It would seem that the police viewed such a notice with scepticism and made no preparation whatsoever to stop any proceedings that might take place on this day.

During Wednesday evening (the 13th), the effigy of Lundy was suspended from the top of Walker's Pillar and the Crimson banner hoisted with the numerals 1688 at its centre. Four Apprentice Boys (James M'Elmun, Philip Shannon, James M'Guire and James Pigott) remained at the Pillar all night, guarding the effigy. As dawn broke the citizens were surprised to see the Crimson flag fluttering from the top of the monument and the effigy of the traitor hanging half-mast against the Pillar. It bore on its breast the well-known words, 'Lundy The Traitor' and on its back 'The End Of All Traitors'. The morning was clear and the crowds of people flocked to the walls as on other civic commemorations. The constabulary authorities were held in complete derision. Dublin Castle at this stage had

Early 19th century engraving of The Shutting of the Gates procession, leaving the Divine service in St Columb's Cathedral and marching down Bishop Street towards the city walls.

19th century engraving of the burning of Lundy from Walker's Pillar.

not yet issued its proclamation prohibiting Apprentice Boys assembling to celebrate the Shutting of the Gates, or the burning of the Lundy effigy. No extra police had been drafted into the City and the effigy was swinging beyond the reach of the police bayonets.

The local authorities realised that it would take some time for a warrant to be issued from Dublin Castle to stop these proceedings.

Just after twelve o'clock, County Inspector Fanning proceeded to the local Petty Sessions Court and taking two of the magistrates off the bench (the Mayor Captain Keogh RM, and Mr Thomas C Cambell JP) went into the private Magisterial Chambers, where a request was drawn up and sent to the Clerk for a warrant to be issued to stop the actions of the Apprentice Boys at Walker's Pillar.

County Inspector Fanning and Sub-Inspector Hogben, under the authority of this warrant, with a posse of constabulary, proceeded to Walker's Pillar. Their purpose was to cut down the effigy of Lundy that had been placed there during late Wednesday evening. They found the gates to the Walker Bastion chained. They snapped them and forced their way round to the door at the back of the Pillar. It too was fastened and barricaded inside, but with the help of a crowbar and sledge they broke the door down and gained access to the Pillar. The cheering crowd, which had gathered on the walls raised the alarm and the four Apprentice Boys who were at the top of the Pillar sprang into action. They pulled the Lundy to the top of the Pillar and set it alight before lowering it again, and by the time the police reached the Pillar summit, Lundy was burned out. They quickly removed the Crimson flag and lowered the flagpole, placing it across the railing at the top of the Pillar. The Lundy skeleton was hauled up to the top of the Pillar and the names of the four Apprentices were noted by the Head Constable O'Connell. Then the four Apprentice Boys descended, carrying with them the skeleton of Lundy along with the ropes and chains used to suspend him from the top. On leaving the Bastion the four men received hearty congratulations from their friends and loud cheers from the assembled crowd, which dispersed, leaving the Pillar in the hands of the police.

The Troubles which occurred over those two years (1870-1871) seem to have been perpetuated by the local MP for the City, Mr Dowse. He was greatly supported in the Parliamentary election by Mr John O'Donnell, a nationalist publican. He had formed another nationalist group in the City called the 'Physical Force Society'. This was totally opposed to the Apprentice Boys Celebrations. No objection was raised by the Protestant community when the City's Catholic community celebrated with great pomp the Pope's twenty-fifth anniversary, or during the St Patrick's Day Celebrations; but now pressure was being placed by Catholic Nationalism on the Executive Government in Dublin to take action against party demonstrations, which could potentially result in disturbances in the City. The Executive Government, in Dublin decided to issue the following document, which was posted on the walls of the City early on Saturday morning:

"BY THE LORD LIEUTENANT-GENERAL AND GENERAL GOVERNOR OF IRELAND.

A PROCLAMATION.

Spencer-Whereas the Mayor and other Magistrates of the City of Londonderry have made requisition of a large civil and military force in order to preserve and prevent a violation of the peace on the 18th inst., on which day divers persons contemplate holding certain assemblies, processions, and displays in the said City; and whereas as assemblies, passions, and displays of a similar character have on former occasions led to and resulted in serious breaches of the peace and produced animosity and ill-will between divers and large numbers of her Majesty's subjects in the said City and its neighbourhood; and whereas we have reason to believe that any such assemblage, procession, or display on the said 18th inst, is calculated to lead to and will be productive of serious breaches of the peace and riot, and also of ill-will and animosity among her Majesty's subjects in the said City and neighbourhood: Now, we, the Lord Lieutenant-General and General Governor of Ireland, in order to prevent any violation of the peace of the said City and neighbourhood and to preserve and maintain good will amongst her Majesty's subjects, do hereby strictly caution and forewarn all persons whomsoever that they do abstain from taking part in or encouraging or inciting to any such assemblage, procession, or display, as aforesaid, in the said City of Londonderry, or in, and on, or about the walls thereof on the said 18th inst. And we do hereby give notice that if, in defiance of this proclamation, any such assemblage, procession, or display shall be attempted or take place, all persons taking part in the same, or encouraging, or inciting thereto, will be proceeded against according to law. And we do hereby order and enjoin all Magistrates and officers entrusted with the preservation of the public peace, and all others whom it may concern, to aid and assist in the due and proper execution of the law in preventing any such assemblage, procession, or display, as aforesaid, and effectually dispersing and suppressing the same, and detecting and prosecuting all persons who after this notice shall offend in the respects aforesaid. Given at her Majesty's Castle of Dublin, this 15th Day of December, 1871. – By his Excellency's command. T. H. Burke."

"God Save the Queen"

The influx of constabulary and military into the City from various parts of Ireland for the 18th sent a clear message to the Apprentice Boys Association that this time their Celebrations would be stopped at all costs. A troop and a half of the First Royal Dragoons (totalling 70) were billeted in various licensed houses that still had stables. Officers in charge were Captain Allan Maclean and Lieutenant Mark Maunsell. The constabulary was headed up by the Assistant Inspector-General Thomas Marcus Brownrigg Esq.

On Saturday afternoon a private meeting was called by the local magistrates in the Mayor's Office in the Corporation Hall. This meeting helped to formalise a strategy plan of how best to utilise crown forces in key locations where disturbances might occur. The use of the Corporation Hall by the Apprentice Boys was discussed. As technically they did not breach the proclamation, it was agreed that they could use the Hall. The constabulary had different plans and took charge of the building, placing some of their men on the roof to prevent a repeat of last year's dilemma – one problem solved!

The Apprentice Boys also held a private meeting on the Saturday evening in their Club Rooms on Church Wall. They too made plans for the Monday Celebrations, considering the proclamation issued by the Lord Lieutenant. Among those who were present at this meeting was the champion of the loyal Orders, Mr William Johnston MP for Belfast and a member of the Apprentice Boys of Derry Murray Club.

Dr Alexander, during his address in the Cathedral, appealed for calm and for all restraint for the 18th Celebration. Dr Kelly at the morning

Mass in the Long Tower Church counselled his hearers to abstain from taking part in any demonstrations and let the authorities deal with the Apprentice Boys.

The dawning of the 18th was ushered in by the Cathedral joy bells and the hoisting of the Crimson flag over the chancel window of the Cathedral. The policemen (armed) paced the wet, slippery streets all night, and from twelve o'clock onwards occasional discharge of small cannon could be heard over the City. Police intelligence tried in vain to locate where the cannon fire was coming from. As soon as they arrived in one location, fire could be heard in the opposite direction. They were fighting a losing battle! The police also acted on a tip off that the effigy of Lundy was to be burned in Pump Street. Arriving at the street, they set up a guard, all of them armed with rifles and fixed bayonets. They stood outside of the Sentinel Office, where it was believed the Traitor would be suspended across the street awaiting its fate.

Shortly before twelve o'clock, Mr John Rea from Belfast, the legal advisor of the Apprentice Boys, and Mr Thomas Mooney, Secretary, came down Bishop Street, where they were joined by Mr William Johnston MP, who was residing at Mr Beatty's, which was a few yards from the entrance to the Corporation Hall. On their arrival at the entrance of the Corporation Hall, they met up with the City's Surveyor, Mr J W McArthur, whose office was located in the Hall. All four were denied access by Mr Redmond RM, who was in charge of the police in this location. All tried to gain access by force and all were pushed back by the constabulary, who then firmly closed the Hall doors in their face. During Mr Rea's discussions with the Police at the Hall doors, he was frequently interrupted by a number of residents from the Bogside, who had made their way up to the top of Butcher Street and were shouting at him to shut up!

There was great excitement and the atmosphere intensified among the gathered crowds, from the Corporation Hall right the whole way up Bishop Street and into the Cathedral grounds. Even the drizzling wet weather could not dampen the spirits of the thousands who had gathered on the footpath in Bishop Street behind the cordon of police and military (mounted and on foot). All the upper windows of the houses in Bishop Street were occupied by eager spectators. It would seem that an earlier address delivered by Mr John O'Donnell to the *'Catholics of Ulster'* to flood into the City for this parade had fallen on deaf ears: the crowd was small and only the occasional nationalist could be seen flaunting a green ribbon. The Police remained posted at Walker's Pillar and had also taken control of an old factory near the walls, where tools and materials were being stored for the rebuilding of the Chapel of Ease (St Augustine's Church).

Having been denied access to the Corporation Hall, Mr Johnston MP, Mr Rea, Mr Mooney and other Apprentices who had met up with them, formed up, donned their crimson sashes and proceeded to march up Bishop Street to the Cathedral for the Divine Service.

As they did so, they were attacked by mounted police, who tried to break up their procession. Again, and again the Apprentices re-formed and pushed their way through via London Street to the Pump Street entrance to the Cathedral. Having safely arrived inside the railings of the Cathedral gates, the Apprentice Boys turned and flaunted their sashes at the police in defiance, where they were also greeted by small cannon fire. About the same time another procession by the Independent Crimson Defenders Club formed in Chapel Lane and, headed by members of the Maiden City Band wearing their uniforms, marched without interruption to the Cathedral via St Columb's Court. Inside the Cathedral was full to capacity and Reverend William Anderson AM of Upper Cumber was the guest preacher, who reminded his hearers of the importance of demonstrating the virtues of Christian living in an age of adversity. The service concluded with the organist playing '*God Bless the Prince of Wales*'.

This was the first time that the Governor of the Association, Mr John Guy Ferguson was absent from the Celebration: this was due to ill health.

On leaving the Cathedral, the Apprentice Boys and friends entered into the Infant School Rooms adjoining the Cathedral for the purpose of holding their usual public meeting. The police authorities could not enter the building without the permission of the Bishop, as the school was still on Church property. Mr Philip Shannon, President of the Association Clubs, presided as the Chairman of the meeting. Speeches criticised the appalling behaviour of the Government at Dublin Castle and that of the local Magistrates, bolstered up by the nationalists and orthodox Presbyterian alliance that existed in the City.

But what of Lundy? The Apprentice Boys had managed thus far to carry out quite a part of their programme; to burn Lundy would truly be an act of defiance in the face of adversity. Between three and four o'clock a large crowd assembled in Bishop Street, with intense activity among the police and military who were trying to prepare for what was going to happen next. The constabulary searched Foy's old coach factory, believing the Lundy to be there. They also searched several other locations, but their efforts proved to be unfruitful. It was only at the twilight hour that Lundy was discovered, not by the police but by hundreds of cheering spectators who thronged the lower part of Bishop Street into the Diamond and at the top of Shipquay Street. There the Lundy was suspended from the end of a plank thrust through a window on the top flat of the house of the former proprietor of the Guardian newspaper (a building that was directly opposite the principal police station), having been set on fire inside and afterwards pushed out through the window. The reaction of the police was slow and by the time they managed to clear a way to the effigy, it had burned out. No arrests were made and by ten o'clock the streets of the City were once again peaceful. Responsibility for building Lundy lay with the Independent Crimson Defender's Club. The Apprentice Boys were yet again victorious, despite Dublin's best efforts to stamp out the 18th Celebrations.

Solidarity within the ranks of the Apprentice Boys has at times been questioned and tested by its own disillusioned members. At the Shutting of the Gates Celebration in 1875, Mr Philip Shannon, President of the Association Clubs and who played a prominent part in the 1871 Celebrations, supported the leadership of Mr Guy Ferguson, the Governor of the Association, whereas Mr John Eakin stated that it was time for Mr Guy Ferguson to stand aside and let someone else lead the Apprentice Boys. The effects of this dispute were clearly demonstrated when members gathered at the Corporation Hall at eleven o'clock for the purpose of marching up Bishop Street to the Cathedral for the Divine Service. Two distinct processions formed up, one marched to the Cathedral, the other marched a different route and at a different time. Records report that Mr Guy Ferguson remained Governor of the Association up to 1888, where his last great act as Governor was to hand over the two renewed Siege flags captured at Windmill Hill on 4th June 1689, to the Dean of the Cathedral on 18th December 1888. The two flags were made of pure white silk and were six feet six inches wide and eight feet six inches long. The tassels were of real gold, with a military skirt of five and a half inches wide. Three fleur de lis worked in gold were embroidered on each flag; both flags were mounted on their original poles captured at Windmill Hill in 1689. The outcome of the usurper Mr Eakin's action remains unknown; he certainly is not mentioned again as having any association with the Apprentice Boys of Derry Organisation.

Thirteen years had lapsed since the Liberal Government of 1871 used force to try to ban the 18th Celebrations. Their acts were pronounced by Lord Chief Justice Whiteside to be arbitrary and illegal, paying the penalty for their indiscretion in a court of law. But by 1883 the Lord Lieutenant-General and General of Ireland, Spencer, and the Government sought to enforce a ban on all parades in the City, by implementing the new 'Prevention of Crime (Ireland) Act 1882'. This was a kneejerk reaction instigated by the action of the National League, who had been involved in several murders of those who opposed their agenda in Ulster. It now threatened to hold a monster Nationalist demonstration on Tuesday 18th December 1883 in Londonderry. So, on Thursday 13th December 1883 the Lord Lieutenant-General and General of Ireland, Spencer, issued the following proclamations:

"By the Lord Lieutenant-General and General of Ireland – Spencer – Whereas, it has been made to appear unto us that a number of persons proposed, and intend, on or about Tuesday the 18th December 1883, to meet and assemble together at the Mall Wall and Royal Bastion, in the City of Londonderry, or elsewhere in, or in the neighbourhood of, the said City, or in the neighbourhood thereof. And, whereas, we have reason to believe that the said meeting and procession, if held would be dangerous to the public peace. Now we, the Lord Lieutenant-General and General Governor of Ireland, under and by virtue of 'the Prevention of Crime (Ireland) Act 1882', and of every other power or authority in that behalf us thereunto enabling, do hereby prohibit the building of the said meetings and procession, whereof all persons

as hereby warned to take notice. Given at Dublin Castle 13th day of December, 1883. God Save the Queen."

"By the Lord Lieutenant-General and General of Ireland – Spencer – Whereas, it has been made to appear unto us that a meeting described by the promoters thereof as a monster National demonstration, is to be held on or about Tuesday 18th December, 1883, at or in the neighbourhood of, the City of Londonderry. And, whereas, we have reason to believe that the said meeting, if held, would be dangerous to the public peace. Now the Lord Lieutenant-General and General of Ireland, under and by virtue of 'the Prevention of Crime (Ireland) Act 1882', and of every other power or authority in that behalf us thereunto enabling, do hereby prohibit the hold of the said meeting, whereof all persons as hereby warned to take notice. Given at Dublin Castle 13th day of December, 1883. God Save the Queen."

Both proclamations were posted throughout the City on the Saturday and later that evening a meeting of the Magistrates and local representatives (Mr John S Macleod RM, Mr Henry Thynne RM, Mr Alderman Darcus (Mayor), Mr Robert McVickers (Mayor-elect), Mr William Tillie, Mr William Bigger, Mr T C Cambell, Mr P T Rodger, Mr Brownrigg, Country Inspector, and Mr Bernard, District Inspector) was held in the Mayor's Office in the Diamond, to consolidate plans to enforce the Bans' success. This meeting also appointed the location of each magistrate in the City and their overall power to utilise the constabulary under their control during Tuesday's 18th Celebration. A force of 250 extra constabulary was drafted into the City from various parts of Ireland, plus 120 men from the 2nd Battalion Royal Welsh Regiment under the command of Colonel Rawlins, from Ebrington Barracks.

The Apprentice Boys made their own plans to celebrate the occasion without formally breaking the Ban. On Monday 17th, a colossal figure of Lundy dressed in full military attire wearing a large cock-hat lay across the top of the railing beneath Walker's statue. The Bastion and the Pillar were guarded all night by members of the Apprentice Boys. At nine o'clock a meeting was held in the Apprentice Boys Memorable Hall and those who had gathered were addressed by the Governor. The younger members of the Association were encouraged to not to breach the law by any rash action. They would still go to the Cathedral for their traditional service, but not marching in procession, and return afterwards to the Memorial Hall. The burning of Lundy would take place, followed by the annual anniversary dinner in the Imperial Hotel. Among those who were attending was Lord Claud Hamilton, MP for Liverpool, and Lord Earnest Hamilton.

A deputation from the Nationalist party met with two of the Magistrates, Mr Macleod and Mr Thynne, objecting to the figure of Lundy at the top of the Pillar and to the possible burning of it on the 18th, stating that it was a breach to the Proclamation. The magistrates relayed that there was no proclamation about banning the burning of Lundy; it did however state that all processions were unlawful.

True to tradition, the Apprentice Boys fired their small cannon at midnight to usher in the day. Lundy was lowered down over the top railing, where he hung all day. Crimson flags were hoisted over Walker's statue and on the tower of the Apprentice Boys Memorial Hall. Mitchelburne's Crimson flag also was raised over the chancel of the Cathedral. Whilst the Ban prohibited the playing of any band music, the joy bells of the Cathedral made up for it, ringing from early morning to late afternoon. The morning was wet and unpleasant, but the streets still thronged with visitors who wanted to maintain this important Siege event. The Apprentice Boys had been gathering in the Memorial Hall from eleven o'clock and at twelve o'clock they began to leave the Hall in large groups, making their way to the Cathedral, wearing their regalia under their coats. Once inside the grounds of the Cathedral, they placed their regalia outside their overcoats; cheering crowds greeted them, as they made their way into the Cathedral for the Divine Service.

Once the service had concluded, the Apprentice Boys made their way back to the Memorial Hall for their customary meeting, which was chaired by the Governor, Mr John Ferguson, who congratulated them on their dignified behaviour both to and from the Cathedral. Several dignitaries voiced their revulsion at the behaviour of the Mayor and Magistrates in the City. Once the meeting had concluded, the crowd made their way on to the walls, which already thronged with spectators. The three Apprentice guardians, who had occupied the Pillar since Sunday, took control of the Lundy effigy and saturated him with petroleum. At three o'clock a rocket was fired from the tower of the Memorial Hall, indicating to the three Apprentice Boys at the top of the Pillar that now was the time to set light to the effigy, which they did. The authorities tried their best to clear the walls and whilst they managed to push the crowds back for the Pillar area, they were unable to completely clear the walls and the surrounding area. The effigy burned for a good ten minutes, and inside the Memorial Hall a band played loyal tunes to those gathered outside during the burning. The crowds quietly dispersed and the streets remained peaceful and no disturbances were reported.

Ensuring the Shutting of the Gates Celebrations remained peaceful and virtually trouble free, and any incidents that did occur remained very minor, allowed both communities to accept each other's culture and traditional annual parades. It was not usual for Catholics to be seen on Derry walls during the burning of Lundy. However, by the early 20th century, Ireland was on the verge of civil war and this was to have an impact on the Apprentice Boys of Derry Association and the City's Orange Order.

Rumours were circulating that the British Government was seriously considering introducing the Home Rule Bill for self-governance in Ireland, much to the delight of the Nationalist people. By 1911 the Government was prepared to repeal the Legislative Union and establish a Parliament in Ireland. The Unionist response like that of the Nationalist, was to establish the Ulster Volunteer Force as a means of protecting Unionist interests in remaining part of the British Parliament, where the Protestant voice would be respected and protected. The signing of the Ulster Covenant by the Unionist community was a clear demonstration of their resolve, united as one in the cause of Protestant liberty and freedom in Ireland. Unity, discipline and self-control was what made the defenders of Derry strong and successful in the past, and now it was time to exhibit those same qualities in the face of opposition. Catholic support was also expressed in terms of maintaining the union with the British Parliament in the South and West of Ireland. At the outbreak of the First World War, many members of the Apprentice Boys joined up to defend their nation's interests, temporarily placing the Ulster Covenant in abeyance until after the war. From 1914 to 1918 the Apprentice Boys maintained the Shutting of the Gates programme, but with the exception that they now had to approach the military, under the Defence of the Realm Act, for permission to burn Lundy on Walker's Pillar. This permission was granted for the ensuing four years of the Great War.

Tensions around Lundy's Day came to a head again in 1919, when Sinn Feiners tried to stir up trouble in and around the Butcher Street

A HISTORY OF THE SHUTTING OF THE GATES CELEBRATIONS 1775-1985

area of the City, by shouting 'Up Dublin,' and 'Up the Rebels'. In Bishop Street, a band returning to their band room was attacked along with some members of the Apprentice Boys Association, but there were no major incidents and the City remained quiet. As a direct result of the rioting that took place in the City in June 1919, the military issued a proclamation prohibiting processions in Londonderry; this proclamation was still in effect by December 1920, but was prescriptive in what the Apprentice Boys could do in celebrating the Shutting of the Gates. The Apprentice Boys complied with the military proclamation which stated, *"... that the movement was not permitted to march their traditional route, nor to burn the effigy of Colonel Robert Lundy from Walker's Pillar."* Instead of the usual procession from the walls to the Cathedral for the Divine Service, they formed up in the grounds of the Cathedral, placed their crimson sashes on and marched around the grounds three times, led by the Britannia Brass and Reid Band who were playing loyal airs. When the Service concluded, the clubs re-formed and again marched around the grounds three times in the presence of a crowded churchyard. The Apprentice Boys returned in small groups to the Memorial Hall through a small military cordon of the Queen's Own West Surrey Regiment, who was drawn across the wall on each side of Walker's Pillar and in Magazine Street, where small groups of Nationalist had started to gather. At four o'clock there was still no sign of Lundy, but the crowd remained optimistic that the Apprentice Boys would not let them down. A horizontal pole appeared at the top of the tower of the Memorial Hall, facing the Society Street side of the Tower. As the Ban only applied to the burning of Lundy from Walker's Pillar and being assured that there would be no military interference, a large Lundy emerged from the Hall doors just after four o'clock and was attached to a chain from the pole on the top of the tower, where it was set alight and hoisted up amidst great cheering and singing from the crowd, who had gathered to witness the burning of Lundy. Lundy burned a good half hour and the whole proceedings concluded with the Britannia Band playing the National Anthem. There was no trouble and the City remained peaceful.

During the remaining years of the 1920s and 1930s, the Shutting of the Gates Celebrations remained quiet, although there was much concern about religious beliefs and cultural identity due to the formation of the new Irish Free State and its impact in Ulster's affairs. A sermon preached by Reverend David Kelly in December 1937 highlighted the importance of not having an unrealistic cultural and religious identity, which the revisionists had revised, but rather an identity that was based on historical facts. He said that:

"When Nationalist spoke of seven hundred years of oppression under British Rule, they must remember it was the Pope who commissioned the English King to rule over Ireland. It ought to be obvious that the Roman Catholic Church was more concerned with the ascendancy of papal temporal power than any eagerness to realise the national aspirations of Irish Republicanism."

The importance of English rule and cultural respectability was further supported by Professor McDonnell of Maynooth, who said, *"The whole burden of my teaching is that apart from England we cannot stand."*

Due to wider world events, the 1940s and 1950s were quiet years in terms of the Shutting of the Gates Celebrations.

However, at the December Lundy Celebrations in 1966, things were about to change. The formation and activities of the Young Republican

Association, who paraded to the Guildhall Square, demanded that the injustice of the homeless and jobless citizens of the Bogside and Creggan be addressed by the City Council. The Diamond was occupied by the Free Presbyterian Church, who held a religious and political meeting and afterwards sold copies to of the Protestant Telegraph to those who had gathered there for the Apprentice Boys Parade. Even though it was reported that there was no trouble at Shutting of the Gates Celebrations, the Apprentices Boys Celebration was about to be highjacked once more by religious politics. Political Lundy's would soon emerge and the Celebrations be seriously opposed. The work of local clergy, calling for religious tolerance and mutual understanding of cultural identity, would soon fall upon deaf ears, and community division would emerge through troubled times, causing division even among some of the Apprentice Boys membership.

The first real threat to the December Celebrations occurred at the beginning of the Troubles era in 1969. On 5th October the Apprentice Boys of Derry Liverpool Branch of the Murray Club had applied for permission to have its annual initiation parade from the Waterside Railway Station to the Apprentice Boys of Derry Memorial Hall, for the initiation of new members into their club. This simple ceremony can only take place within the walls of Londonderry and is usually carried out by the Governor of the Association, who offers to each new member a hand of friendship and welcome into the Association. For the Liverpool Murray Club, these events had their origins in 1964, but on this occasion their application for parading in the City was rejected due to Lord Cameron's Report into the cause of the outbreak of violence and civil disturbance in Northern Ireland since and around 5th October 1968. The Civil Rights Movement in Londonderry also planned a parade to coincide with the Apprentice Boys parade, starting at the Railway station, at the same time and parading along the same route as the one they applied for, the only difference was that instead of parading to the Memorial Hall, they would march around the Diamond and down Shipquay Street and into the Guildhall Square for a rally. The Cameron Report suggested that given the recent disturbance and the many facets that led to and caused the violence on the streets of Northern Ireland, especially in Londonderry, all parades on 5th October 1968 should be banned. This Public Order was issued by Mr William Craig and read as follows:

THE TERMS OF THE MINISTER'S PROHIBITIONS ON MARCHES PUBLIC ORDER ACT NORTHERN IRELAND 1951

WHEREAS, I, The Right Honourable WILLIAM CRAIG, Minister of Home Office Affairs for Northern Ireland, am of opinion that the holding, on Saturday, 5th October, 1968, of any public processions or meetings in certain parts of the County Borough of Londonderry may give rise to serious public disorder:

Now, THEREFORE, I The Right Honourable WILLIAM CRAIG, Minister of Home Office Affairs for Northern Ireland, in exercise of the powers conferred upon me by Section 2(2) of the Public Affairs Act (Northern Ireland) 1951, do hereby order that the holding, on Saturday 5th October 1968, of all public processions or meetings in any public highway, road, street or public place in that part of the County

> Borough of Londonderry situated within and on the walls, and in the Waterside Ward of the said County Borough, be prohibited.

> Wm. Craig
> Minister of Home Affairs
> For Northern Ireland
> 3rd October 1968

The Liverpool Murray Club reacted with decorum, but was dismayed that their parade should be banned because of the actions of Derry's Civil Rights Movement, which had nothing to do with the religious rights, liberty and freedom of all people. The Civil Rights Movement opposed the Ban and paraded, which led to rise of civil disturbance in the City lasting several days. The seeds of discontent sown during these disturbances unsettled communities and the origins of the Troubles can be traced back to such flash points in history.

This Government Ban was still in place as the days drew closer to the December Celebrations, due to the troubles that developed in the Bogside and in Bishop Street after the Breaking of the Boom Celebrations in August 1969. Again, the Apprentice Boys of Derry Celebrations would become strained with the introduction of the British Army onto the streets of Londonderry (1st Battalion of Prince of Wales's Own Regiment of Yorkshire, which was initially based in the old Derry Jail in Bishop Street). The General Committee Members of the Apprentice Boys of Derry under the leadership of Dr W R Abernethy OBE decided to hold a secret meeting in the Memorial Hall, to which the Police Superintendent for the City was invited, to discuss a programme for the 18th Celebrations. The results of this meeting were twofold:

That they would adhere to the Government Ban and not parade in any part of the City on the day. Instead they would gather at the doors of the Cathedral, put on their crimson regalia and parade a Crimson flag up the aisle of the Cathedral during the Divine Service. On completion of the service, they would remove their regalia, put them in their pockets and quietly disperse.

1. The General Committee of the Apprentice Boys Association agreed that there would be no effigy of Lundy made and burned in the City. (This would have been the first time since 1788 that an effigy was not burned in the City at the December Celebrations.)
2. That there would be no annual firing of canon to usher in the 18th morning.

There was sharp division and exchanging of words among members of the Association, who felt that the leadership should have been stronger, displaying the spirit of Siege defenders and pushing for more elements of the Celebrations to be carried out than what was agreed to at the secret meeting in the Memorial Hall with the police.

As the 18th approached, the Army cordoned off all access to the walls around the Walker's Bastion, to prevent the Apprentice Boys from gaining access to the Pillar and breaking the enforced Government Ban. On the eve of the Celebration a number of Apprentice Boys gathered in Lundy's Room in the Memorial Hall. Their intent was to approach the security forces on the walls to gain access to the Pillar to hoist the Crimson flag at the top beside Walker's statue and to raise the Union Jack at the bottom right-hand side of the Bastion. Among those who approached the security forces were Bobby Jackson, Jim Guy, James Mc Clements, and Mr D

Davis. The initial meeting with an army officer in charge of the walls was hostile, but Chief Inspector Jackson from the Strand Road Police Barracks intervened, and assured him that whatever Bobby Jackson said, that is exactly what would happen, as he was to be trusted. After further discussion and assurance, it was agreed that they could fly their flags at the Pillar on the condition that as soon as the Celebration service was over, they would remove them, which they did.

There was much excitement in and around the streets of the Fountain on the eve of Lundy's Day, with Army patrols asking questions of its residents as to the whereabouts of a person called Lundy, who was potentially to be executed the next day.

The General Committee of the Apprentice Boys wholly accepted the official Ban, especially over the burning of Lundy. Some members felt that they displayed weak leadership and did not display the spirit of 1688.

In the weeks leading up to the 18th Celebrations an effigy of Lundy was secretly built in a shed in the Fountain.

The wooden shed in which Lundy was built measured approximately 40 feet in length and was approximately 10 feet wide. The height of the shed measured 13 feet at its highest point with a sloping felt roof to the height of 8 feet at its lowest point. Due to the height of the shed, it was impossible to stand the Lundy effigy up on its feet to dress it, so it was dressed while lying on its back on two trestles. Light in the shed was provided by two paraffin hurricane oil lamps suspended from the wooden ceiling. All the gaps at the front of the shed were sealed up so as not to let any light escape though them into the street. This Lundy was made by members of the Jackson family. The building was partly funded by the Londonderry Division of the Ulster Protestant Volunteers organisation, who gave a cheque of £3 to help cover part of the financial cost in building the effigy of Lundy.

The straw for building the Lundy was provided by a local farmer and a loyal member of the Apprentice Boys Browning Club. The brown sacking and black cloth for Lundy's cloths were bought in Hills of the Strand Road and the wood for his boots and backbone was bought in Balintine's of the Strand Road. One major problem that faced the builders was the issue of Lundy's backbone, a vital part to which the whole sacking and wire structure of Lundy was attached. The backbone on which the traditional Lundy was made was a solid iron bar which stood about ten feet tall with a ring at the top for hanging the effigy up. There were two other cross metal bar sections; one for attaching the two legs and the other one nearer the top for Lundy's head. Two wooden boards were attached by two metal bolts to the flat part of the backbone on which the brown sacking of Lundy's body was attached. An alternative had to be found, so after much planning it was decided that a wooden backbone be made with identical metal cross sections for his legs and head, with a metal flat plate with a ring at the top of the purpose of hanging Lundy up. (This metal plate and ring was made by someone from Killaloo who worked in Craig's Engineering Works in the Strand Road.) Making such a backbone removed the risk of losing the original metal one should the authorities move in to confiscate the Lundy effigy.

This Lundy was made and dressed according to the normal pattern of past effigies, except on this occasion it only stood at fifteen feet, making it easy to move and to handle when the 18th Celebrations arrived. Prior to Lundy's Day, and in keeping with Apprentice Boys tradition, the noise of a canon was heard in the Fountain area of the City. This cannon was privately owned and was fired in the back yard of Logue's Builders Merchants in Fountain Street. Both the Police and Army made a search of the lower Fountain area to try and find out where it was fired from and to apprehend the culprits, but their search was in vain.

On the morning of the 18th, Crimson flags flew from Walker's Pillar, the Cathedral, the Apprentice Boys Memorial Hall and several houses in the Fountain. Security was tight especially in Society Street, London Street, Bishop Street, the Fountain and the general area around the Cathedral Churchyard. The security forces did have some concerns about what the radical element of the Apprentice Boys might do, but they never once suspected that a Lundy effigy was made and ready for burning at the appointed time, namely four o'clock.

Apprentice Boys attending the annual Divine Service in the Cathedral put on their regalia after entering the Church. Many other Apprentices refused to attend or associate themselves with the Leadership of the Association, as they disagreed with their decision.

Once the service ended, Apprentices who had attended the service removed their regalia at the church doors and dispersed. At approximately four o'clock, as some of the Apprentice Boys leaders (the Lieutenant-Governor Mr W S Heatley, General Secretary Mr James Mc Clements, Mr Tommy Diver and other Apprentice Boys Officers and members) were returning to their homes in the Fountain, the effigy of Lundy borne on three wooden batons was carried by six men to the end of Clarence Place. Another man was in possession of a large wooden ladder, while a third person had a chain with a hook at one end to attach to the ring at the top of Lundy head. Their task was to hang the burning Lundy from one of the metal bars from one of the portholes on the top of New Gate. What they did not anticipate was that Lundy caught fire very quickly and that it would have been impossible to carry out their plans successfully. Instead they had to drop the burning Lundy near New Gate at the junction of Hawking Street and the Fountain, to the cheers of around a hundred people, who were singing '*The Sash*' and other loyal songs. Some of those who had gathered had crimson sashes on, and as the returning members of the Apprentice Boys walked past the burning Lundy, the crowd call out to them, "Traitors!" Two soldiers were manning an Army sentry box at the junction of Hawking Street and lower Fountain Street, but were powerless to do anything, nor were they sure what was happening in front of them. No arrests were made and the crowd cleaned up the remains of Lundy's burnt out frame. This was the only time in the history of burning Lundy that the effigy was burned outside the City walls. Bobby Jackson and his associates were hailed as heroes and champions of the Protestant cause, while the actions and credibility of the Governor and General Committee members of the Apprentice Boys Association did much damage to the Association's reputation among the loyalist community.

The introduction of the Government Ban in 1968 was to last to December 1971, although there were some concessions made by the security forces about the contents of the Celebrations. In 1970 a compromise was reached between the security forces and the Apprentice Boys in that they were permitted to fly their flags from Walker's Pillar, but not to burn an effigy of Lundy from it, as it might cause a reaction from the residents in the Bogside, which potentially could lead to violence. They were also granted permission to fire their small cannon at the steps leading up onto the walls opposite the Memorial Hall. However, the decision by the security forces not to allow Lundy to be burned from the Pillar was not revealed until late on the 16th evening, leaving the Apprentice Boys with a difficult decision as to where to burn an eighteen-foot Lundy.

The Lundy builders had a solution for the situation. While they were constructing the normal size effigy for Walker's Pillar, they had also made a further Lundy about fourteen feet high for the Londonderry Division of the Ulster Protestant Volunteers Force, to be burned in Limavady, as the Apprentice Boys there decided to adhere to the Government Ban. The Lundy for the Londonderry UPV was constructed in a shed, but when it came to dressing him in his military uniform, members of the UPV secretly carried the effigy out of the shed on three batons to McKay's old gateway in Fountain Street. There they were able to stand Lundy upright and dressed him over two nights. When completed he was secretly carried back to shed to await collection.

The Apprentice Boys General Committee, knowing about this second Lundy, exchanged the Londonderry one for the smaller Lundy, who was transported to the Memorial Hall on the back of a lorry. This same lorry then transported the eighteen-foot Lundy to Limavady for burning on the 18th night.

As the 18th fell on a Saturday, it was decided in 1970 by the General Committee of the Apprentice Boys to move the burning of Lundy in future days to the Saturday nearest the 18th, which would enable other Apprentice Boys members throughout Northern Ireland to participate in the Celebrations without having to lose a day's pay from work.

On Friday 17th, the authorities permitted the Apprentice Boys of Derry to switch on the new spotlights placed at the four corners of Walker's Bastion shining up onto the Pillar and statue of Reverend George Walker at the top. The Crimson flag was hoisted at the top of the Pillar and the Union Jack flew at the bottom right-hand side of the Bastion. Walker's statue was draped with a large crimson sash. As midnight approached several small canon shots rang out over the City, Lundy's Day had arrived!

Four hundred extra police were drafted into the City for the Celebrations, where they were strategically placed at street corners, on the walls and around the Memorial Hall and by the Cathedral. On the Saturday morning prior to the Divine Service in the Cathedral, several new members were initiated into the Apprentice Boys of Derry Association at a special ceremony in the Memorial Hall, Society Street.

From early morning some of the Apprentice Boys, along with some of the Lundy builders and Mr D Portor, assembled a twenty-foot-high free-standing tubular steel scaffolding square in the car park of Society Street, for the purpose hanging and burning Lundy on it. At twelve o'clock the fourteen-foot Lundy was carried out of Lundy's Room in the Memorial Hall to the erected scaffold, which was placed by the old Corporation storehouse house at the corner of the car park in Society Street, facing the Memorial Hall.

Church Bastion was also seen as a viable place to burn Lundy as it overlooked the Protestant Fountain Street and also could be seen from the Cathedral churchyard. The chief reason why this site was rejected was due to the size of scaffold need for the people in the Fountain to actually see Lundy hanging on it.

By now it was estimated that a crowd of one thousand people had gathered into the car park area to witness the burning of Lundy. The effigy was put on the hook in the centre of the scaffold to secure it, so as to prevent any accidents occurring. By now there was great excitement among the gathered crowd, who were singing loyal songs and enjoying the occasion.

Before the torch was applied to light Lundy, a struggle took place with some members of the Apprentice Boys from Belfast, who wanted to push the scaffold with Lundy hanging on it over towards the walls. The scaffold with Lundy on it almost fell upon the crowd, and at this stage some police officers moved in to try and take control of the situation. Just as they were doing so, Lundy's boots were set on fire and the situation calmed down. As Lundy burned, the pealing of the bells of the Cathedral could be heard playing hymns and other tunes to commemorate the occasion

The burning of Lundy lasted thirty minutes, and when he was reduced to ashes, the Governor and members of the General Committee, accompanied by fellow brethren with regalia on made their way in groups to the Cathedral Church for their annual Divine Service. The preacher was the Reverend James Clarke, who during his address reminded his listeners of the importance of remembering great events from the past, especially the acts of their forefathers during the siege of 1688-89, and that accusations of bigotry, or extremism and coat-trailing were not conducive labels leading to building and developing good community relationships. This was the first and last time in the history of the 18th Celebrations that Lundy was burned before the Divine Service in the Cathedral. Not all members of the Apprentice Boys Association were willing to accept the Ban imposed upon them. Earlier in the day, a band accompanied by members of the Apprentice Boys of Derry from Belfast, marched from their parked buses in Spencer Road, broke ranks and marched around the police cordon on Craigavon Bridge, and continued to parade up Hawking Street, over London Street and into Society Street, stopping outside the Apprentice Boys Memorial Hall. After the burning of Lundy, they reformed and paraded from Society Street to Spencer Road, accompanied by eight police land rovers, two abreast, that prevented them from marching down Pump Street, Artillery Street and Lower Fountain Street. The police made no arrests of those who defied the Ban and the Celebrations passed off peacefully.

In 1971, the Ban was still in place preventing the Apprentice Boys from parading their traditional route from the Apprentice Boys Memorial Hall to St Columb's Cathedral for the Divine Service. The security forces gave permission for Walker's Pillar to be decorated in the usual manner. The ancient walls were now closed to the public and all entrances were blocked by barbed wire and picket posts driven into the ground. The churchyard of St Augustine's facing Walker's Pillar was also heavily wired off to the height of ten feet, again blocking all access to the City walls. The only access that the Apprentice Boys had was through St Augustine's churchyard, the Army having the keys for both the church gates and access to the Walker's Pillar. They met the Army at the church gates and were escorted to the Royal Bastion to hoist the Crimson flag at the top of the Pillar and the Union Jack at the bottom right-hand corner. As the eighteen foot flagpole was being raised at the bottom of the Pillar, several shots were fired up at the Bastion, but no one was hurt and the Army did not return fire. Having completed this part of the preparation for Lundy's Day on the Saturday, the Apprentices then went to the Memorial Hall and prepared the two small brass canons for firing at midnight. As midnight approached a small crowd gathered to see the cannons being fired. Both police and Army were present, so as to prevent any incidents occurring. The canons were fired at the steps leading up to the walls and the crowd dispersed peacefully.

As dawn approached, Crimson flags were hoisted on the Memorial Hall, the Cathedral and several houses in the Fountain. The Bells of the Cathedral played hymns and other appropriate tunes in keeping with the occasion, as members of the Apprentice Boys gathered from various parts of Northern Ireland for the Celebration. Due to the trouble that occurred at the previous burning of Lundy, the General Committee of the Apprentice Boys decided that a new location needed to be found. For purposes of security and containment, New Gate at the end of London Street was the chosen location. The City walls were still closed to the public but a few key members of the Apprentice Boys were permitted access up onto New Gate, where an eighteen-foot steel girder was placed out over the third porthole and weighted down at the other end with heavy sandbags. At the protruding end of the girder a pulley hook was fixed on which the fourteen-foot Lundy was hung. Again, the Lundy was made by the Jacksons, dressed in his traditional uniform, and dangled for most of the day in McKay's Gateway, guarded by some Apprentice Boys and members of the security forces. This new location for the burning of Lundy worked well for the Apprentice Boys, who after the Divine Service, with Crimson flags and regalia on, walked the short distance down through the Cathedral churchyard and onto London Street to New Gate for the burning of Lundy. Prior to the Apprentice Boys leaving the Cathedral churchyard, a new addition was added to the Celebrations, namely the placing of a wreath of crimson flowers on the mound of the Siege Heroes. As the Campsie Parent Club was responsible for all the arrangements for the Celebration for 1971, the President of the Club, Mr Norman Millar, was the first to place a wreath on the mound, thus starting a tradition that continues up to this very day. When the General Committee of the Apprentice Boys arrived at New Gate, Mr Bobby Jackson made a short speech,

> "It gives me great pleasure on behalf of the Citizens of this unconquered City to present you with this stick to light the effigy of Colonel Robert Lundy."

At that, he presented the stick to the Governor of the Apprentice Boys, Mr J McClements, who in turn gave it to Mr Peden McKee, Secretary of the Campise Parent Club. Bobby then lit the end of the stick and Mr McKee lit the bottom of Lundy's legs, just above his boots. As he did so a great cheer went up from the crowd, who starting to sing *'Derry Walls'* and similar songs. The Lundy effigy burned for a good thirty minutes, after which the crowd dispersed and the remains of the effigy were removed. During the day several shots rang out in the direction of the City walls, no one was hurt, and again Bobby Jackson and his team of Apprentices removed the flags from the top and bottom of Walker's Pillar. The City remained quiet and no arrests were made during the Celebrations.

The Government Ban which had been in place for several years was lifted 1972, allowing the Apprentice Boys to parade from the Memorial Hall to the Cathedral for the annual Divine Service. The Parade was led by the Hamilton Flute Band and a contingent from Belfast was led by the David Sales Flute Band, Belfast. They marched through the streets inside the walls and through Ferryquay Gate into Carlisle Road, and then via Hawking Street to the Cathedral. At the conclusion of the service, a wreath was placed on the Apprentice Boys Mound in the Cathedral churchyard by Mr Thomas Lynn, Chaplain elect for the Murray Parent Club. The parade then re-formed in the churchyard and marched the short distance to New Gate where the effigy of Lundy hung all day. The torch was applied to the effigy by Mr T Lynn. As the effigy burned out, the Belfast Branch, led by their band, marched down Hawking Street and over to the Waterside to their buses. The Murray Club from Belfast presented two new Crimson flags, one to the Memorial Hall and the other to be flown at the top of Walker's Pillar. The only confrontation of the day was instigated by a small tartan group, where two of them were moved on by the police.

1973 was not a good year for the Apprentice Boys Association. Their beloved Walker's Pillar had been destroyed by a bomb in August of that year. Only the plinth was left, but as the approaching Shutting of the Gates Celebrations drew near, Mr D Portor was approached by the General Committee to fix a new flagpole to the plinth, so that the traditional Crimson flag could be hoisted on the Pillar. Mr Portor carried out the work and both traditional flags were flown in their proper positions, i.e. the crimson on the Pillar Plinth and the Union Jack in its normal position at the bottom right-hand corner. Lundy was again burned at New Gate and the wreath on the Apprentice Boys Mound was placed there by Mr Stewart Heatley, Past President of the Apprentice Boys of Derry Parent Club. One factor that stands out about this year's programme was that the parade was much longer than usual. It formed up at the Apprentice Boys Memorial Hall and paraded down Bishop Street, the Diamond, Ferryquay Street, Carlisle Road and Hawking Street to the Cathedral. The return parade followed the same route to New Gate where Lundy was set on fire by Mr Thomas Diver, Secretary of the Apprentice Boys of Derry Parent Club. On the Friday morning the cremated remains of Mr George Roberts a veteran of the Liverpool Murray Club, were interned in the Apprentice Boys Mound in the Cathedral churchyard. Before his death Mr Robert requested that his earthly remains should be buried within the historic walls of Derry. The Dean of Derry, Reverend George Good, was approached about the possibility of having them buried in the Apprentice Boys Mound, and the Dean granted their request. A number of Apprentice Boys gathered for the burial, with their crimsons on. The Dean conducted the short service and Mr Bobby Jackson, the Verger of the Cathedral, filled in the grave. Unlike the previous year, there was no trouble throughout Lundy's day.

The 18th Celebrations in 1974 witnessed real trouble. This took place in the Diamond, Butcher Street area of the City, where a crowd of youths had gathered and started to stone the returning parade as it made its way up to Bishop Street toward the new burning position for Lundy, opposite the Courthouse and the Masonic Hall. This was the first Lundy to be made in six years in Lundy's own room in the Apprentice Boys Memorial Hall. This Lundy stood eighteen feet high, the size of the original Lundy who hung from Walker's Pillar before its destruction in 1973. Again, the effigy was hung on a large scaffold from early morning. Members of the Apprentice Boys along with members of the security forces guarded the effigy in case someone might attempt to set fire to it. All of the normal 18th customs were observed, from the firing of cannon, to the hoisting of flags on Walker's Plinth, the Cathedral, Memorial Hall and the Victoria Hall in Spencer Road. What was noticeable was that the number of Apprentice Boys marching and bands had increased, along with the crowds that had flocked into the City for the day.

In 1981, the crowd attending the burning of Lundy had risen to over two thousand accompanied by several bands from all parts of Northern Ireland, and the protests by Nationalists became fewer. The Apprentice Boys of Derry Association has done much over the past years to become more inclusive of all communities within the City, promoting education as a means to greater understanding of what the Association is about and why their traditions are so important to the Protestant community, and the implications of what the Siege of 1688-89 achieved, namely religious freedom for all people.

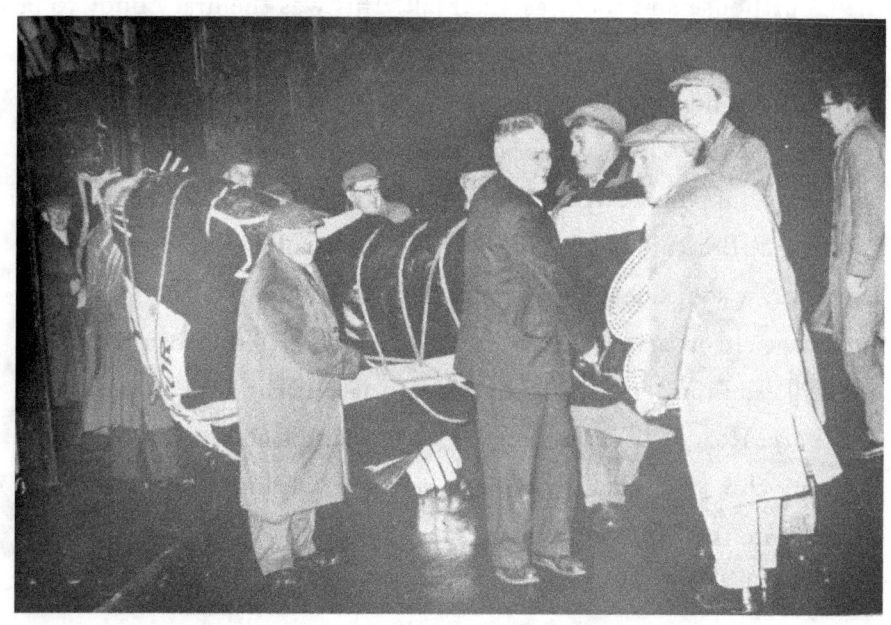

An early morning call, Apprentices help carry the effigy of Lundy from the Apprentice Boys memorial Hall to Walker's Pillar in the 60's.

CHAPTER 4
THEIR CANNONS DID ROAR!

The use of canon fire to celebrate Apprentice Boys of Derry anniversaries is not something new. Cannon salutes had their origins in ancient practices, indicating that a battle was over and that an instrument which had caused so much pain and destruction, was now firing blank shots as a celebratory demonstration that the battle had been won. The Apprentice Boys of Derry Association which commemorated two anniversary events by the firing of cannon, did so not to offend or persecute their neighbours but to celebrate that difficult times were over.

The earliest account of cannon salutes in Londonderry was after the great Siege of 1688-89. The occasion was the arrival of General Percy Kirk to the City on the 4th August 1689. He was received at Bishop Gate by the joint Governors of the City (Reverend George Walker and Colonel John Mitchelburne) and other Civic officials, to the thunderous roar of cannon from the ramparts. A gap of several years occurred before the next official record of cannon fire to celebrate the ending of the Siege of 1689. This was organised on 1st August 1718 by Colonel John Mitchelburne along with several similar-spirited defenders. Records state that the Reverend William Nicolson (who was newly appointed Bishop of Derry) read prayers in the Cathedral, Mitchelburne's Crimson flag was raised on the Cathedral, while in the afternoon cannon fire and volleys of shots could be heard resounding around the City walls and beyond.

June 12th 1778 witnessed the formation of the Mitchelburne Volunteers, which consisted of tradesmen who formed the third company of The Independent Company of Volunteers in the City. They were militarily disciplined. An advertisement in the Londonderry Journal on Tuesday 14th July 1778, states that an Apprentice Boys Company also formed part of the Independent Volunteers, under the command of Captain William Lecky, Esq, and Captain Stephen Bennett, Esq, and that they fired three volleys (musket fire) at the four gates and in the Diamond, during the Celebration of the City's Two Big Days.

The 1788 Centenary Celebration witnessed a discharge of twenty-one guns fired from the ramparts. The battleship Porcupine, as it approached the quay, responded with an equal number of cannon discharges. In 1797, when the Londonderry Legion were presented with their new pair of Regimental Colours as part of the December Celebrations by Brigadier-General the Earl of Cavan, the artillery fired a twenty-one gun salute and the infantry three volleys in honour of the day. A gap appears in the firing of cannon from 1797 until 18th December 1813, when smaller field pieces were fired at the four Gates to usher in the day. This happened to coincide with the laying of the foundation stone of the new Court House in Bishop Street. Again, a further gap appears in the history of cannon firing until 1822, when the City Corporation decided that the old pieces of ordinance that were sunk on the quays should be taken up and replaced on the ramparts. The famous Fishmonger's Gun, better known as the Roaring Meg, was placed on a new gun carriage and was put into complete working order by the Apprentice Boys, and was used for ushering in the

Two Big Days until 1832. The Apprentice Boys mentioned in 1822 in all probability belonged to the Apprentice Boys of Derry Club that was established in 1814. It took a leading part in both Siege Commemorations after Colonel Pearson's interference with the Londonderry Yeomanry in 1821. This Club was not only responsible for firing the Roaring Meg, but they were the first Apprentice Boys of Derry Club to purchase a small field cannon, which they fired at each of the four City gates, during the Siege Celebrations. This Club also carried a royal standard. This had been presented by Lady Louisa Connelly to the Glendermott Volunteers some forty years earlier. Their place in the procession to celebrate the Shutting of the Gates was directly behind the Londonderry Yeomanry. In 1823, this Club had a membership of fifty young men who took the lead in firing the first shots at each of the four gates at the 18th Celebration.

In October 1824, a new Apprentice Boys of Derry Club was formed which called itself '*The No Surrender Club*'. This swelled the number of Apprentices on parade in December of that year to over one hundred members. The Londonderry Journal records that the Apprentice Boys ushered in the dawning of the day by firing several rounds from the Roaring Meg.

By 1838, the Apprentice Boys of Derry Clubs (The No Surrender No 1 & No 2; the Death and Glory Club and the Reformed) owned five small field pieces, mounted on beautiful wooden two-wheeled gun carriages, which fired on the evening and during the morning part of the 18th Celebrations. By 1839, the number of cannons increased to eight and prior to the Divine Service on the 18th, these guns were deposited of in the Apprentice Boys Club Rooms dotted around the City, the largest being situated in the Linen Hall, Rosemary Street. It was from this location that the Apprentice Boys formed up prior to parading around the walls and up to the Cathedral in 1831. The Linen Hall would remain the primary rallying point for all of the Apprentice Boys Clubs to gather, form up, parade and return to, for the Divine Service in the Cathedral for both Siege Celebrations until 1854, when the focus was then switched to the Corporation Hall in the Diamond.

Cannon have been used for the 18th Celebrations since the inception of the Apprentice Boys of Derry Association. During the early part of the 19th century, this mainly consisted of firing a twenty-one-gun salute from the four principal gates of the City. With the increase in number of field guns to eight in 1839, at seven o'clock on the 18th morning salvos of twenty-four-gun salutes were fired over each of the four principal gates, followed by a firing of a thirty-gun salute on Mall Wall. At the end of this part of the day's proceedings the cannon were paraded down Bishop Street, the Diamond and Shipquay Street to the Linen Hall where the guns were deposited.

This established custom of firing of the ancient cannon was to continue up to 12th August 1840, when one of the ancient cannons exploded, *"killing Thomas Fleming, injuring John Platt, who lost his eyesight by it, and wounding Robert Orr."*[13] On 17th December 1840, the Apprentice Boys issued the following statement in the Londonderry Sentinel:

To the Citizens of Derry

".... Circumstances have occurred, that have rendered it advisable that our usual mode of celebrating that great event by the firing of cannon, should, on this coming occasion, be dispensed with. In obedience to the wishes on many who have co-operated with us; and in the deference to

---

13 Hempton, John. *The Siege and History of Londonderry* (1861) p 450

the expressed opinions of a large portion of our fellow-citizens who have determined not to observe that part of the Celebration to which our partiality has attached much gratification and importance. We have come to this determination with much painful sacrifice of feeling on our part, but in accordance with the opinions of those who are entitled to our consideration and respect. We yield no principles – we abandon no duty – we desert no opinions – for nothing ever has, and nothing ever shall shake our firm lasting, and steadfast adherence to the Derry principle of 'No Surrender.'"

On this occasion the ancient cannons remained silent, but would be used again to usher in the Shutting of the Gates Celebrations the following year and right up to 1856, when it was also decided that for safety reasons the midnight salvo would no longer be fired and that the first canon to be fired on the 18th morning would be to announce the hoisting up of Lundy on Walker's Pillar at five o'clock in the morning. In 1859, the hoisting of Lundy time would also be changed to a more reasonable time of six o'clock. Apart from the Roaring Meg, the ancient cannons used to usher in Lundy's Day were situated in the Royal Bastion. There were three in total.

By 1846, the numbers of field guns that the Apprentice Boys Association owned was nine, and all were stored at the Linen Hall. By 1848 they numbered thirteen, a significant reminder of the brave thirteen who shut the Gates of Derry against the forces of King James in 1688. Because of the significant number of cannons owned by the Association, it was decided in 1848 that they should be divided into two gun batteries. The first division/battery was under the command of John B Henderson, President of the No Surrender Club, who had four guns which were stored in their Club Room which was situated in London Street. The second division of cannon was under the command of Mr James W Gregg, President of Number Three Apprentice Boys of Derry Club. The other Clubs forming this division consisted of the following: The Juvenile Club; the True Blues and the Walker Club. This division had nine guns in total, and these were stored on his premises of Mr Gregg of Pump Street.

By 1844, the Apprentice Boys used their cannon considerably more to celebrate the Big Day, by firing at several key locations. The first firing position was at Mall Wall; this was followed by a further twenty-one-gun salute at the Artillery Bastion and concluded with a final firing at Walker's Pillar. 1848 witnessed the number of cannons owned by the Apprentice Boys increase from eight to nine and were divided into two batteries. The first was commanded by Mr John B Henderson, President of the No Surrender Club, who was in charge of four field cannon taken from their Club Room in London Street to Walker's Pillar. They were joined by Mr William Cregg, President of the Apprentice Boys of Derry Club, who was in charge of the second battery. The Murray Club and the Masters' Foy had their own small field cannon and they joined in the firing with the first battery. The only difference to the normal salvos was that the number of rounds fired per location had diminished to three. This year also introduced further firing of cannon during the burning of Lundy from Walker's Pillar. This was under the command of Mr John B Henderson.

According to C D Milligan, the numbers of field guns owned by each of the Apprentice Boys Club in 1855 were:

"The Apprentice Boys of Derry Club - 2 heavy brass field pieces;
The Walker Club – 3 field pieces;
The Murray Club – 3 field pieces;

The Williamite Club – 3 field pieces;

The Mitchelburne Club – 2 large field pieces."[14]

By 1860, Mr Gregg's premises in Lower Pump Street housed the majority of field guns owned by the Apprentice Boys Association. The exception was with the Mitchelburne Club whose large guns were stored in premises also belonging to Mr Gregg at the top of Pump Street.

However, by 1865 the number of cannons used was reduced to ten, one of them being a new gun purchased by the newly reformed No Surrender Club. Mr John Hempton (President of the Mitchelburne Club) sold a further four cannons to the Association. Two of these six pounders which had been used in previous Celebrations but had not been used for two to three years, were purchased by the Apprentice Boys of Derry and the No Surrender Clubs. One of the other two field guns was probably purchased by the Browning Club, formed in 1861. In the Club's old minutes dated 16th December 1880, there is a mention of, *"The gun we have now belonged to the old Browning Club, and had been buried for the past 11 years."* [15]

There is no record as to who purchased the fourth cannon.

The Williamite Club still existed and was still part of the 18th Celebrations in 1867, but by 1881 they no longer existed. This may well have been due to a small and ageing Club membership or due to an ongoing rift between them and the Murray Club as to their place in order of the parade. It is possible that three of the cannons sold by John Hempton may have been the three field guns that once belonged to the Williamite Club. The fourth cannon seems to have been a new one.

---

14 Milligan C D *The Walker Club Centenary* (1944) p 39
15 Unknown. *Browning Club Apprentice Boys of Derry Centenary of its Revival 1861-1961* p 27

The total cannon in 1865 now numbered fourteen in all, but not all of the guns were used for firing on each of the Celebrations.

Objections to the firing of the Apprentice Boys field pieces first occurred in 1860 under the new Party Emblems Act (1860), which was more stringent than the Anti Processions Act (1832), and outlined five Offences:

1. The publicly exhibiting or displaying upon any building or place, any banner, flag, party emblem or symbol.
2. The wilfully permitting or suffering to be publicly exhibited, or displayed, upon building or place, any banner, flag, party emblem or symbol.
3. The public meeting, and parading, with other persons in any public street, or road.
4. Playing any music, in public street, road or place.
5. Discharging any cannon or firearms in any public street, road or place.

This new Act was a reactionary political attack on the Orange Order over the serious riots that occurred in Derrymacash, near Lurgan, County Armagh.

Even though 600 troops were drafted into the City to stop the usual 18th December Celebrations from taking place, their powers were wasted, as the Apprentice Boys of Derry Association argued that their celebrations were official civic events and were totally separate from the Orange Order, thus making their celebrations legal. Furthermore, as a large number of Roman Catholics joined in to celebrate the Shutting of the Gates and watch the burning of Lundy from Walker's Pillar, it could not be regarded as an act of sectarianism.

The Apprentice Boys Association was divided in their opinion about the firing of their cannons on this occasion. Some felt that it was not necessary to carry out the customary salvos at various parts on the City walls. Others felt that the usual midnight firing of cannon was enough to appease all concerned. When Lundy's day arrived, the Mitchelburne Club, under the direction of Mr James Gregg of Pump Street, brought out the Club gun and proceeded to the walls, where they fired six rounds. Then they returned their field cannon back to its store. No arrests were made nor was any attempt made by the military or police to confiscate the Club's cannon.

Due to political and religious tensions in the City in 1870, attempts were made by the local authorities, backed by a large military and police force, to ban the Apprentice Boys 18th Celebration. This was the first time that the Association decided not to fire their thirteen field guns in fear of them being taken from them by the Authorities. But in order not be out-manoeuvred, and in keeping with tradition as best as they could, the Apprentice Boys fired two shots from a small cannon (a first) at midnight. Despite the best efforts of the police and Army searching all prime locations within the City, the whereabouts of this small cannon could not be found, nor the person or persons who fired it.

The Apprentice Boys Association made a conscious decision in 1885 that in order to adhere to the Peace and Preservation Act, the customary firing of their field guns to usher in the Big Days would cease. However, during the December 1888 Celebration, thirteen field cannons were used in honour of the day. It would seem that this was the last date that the Apprentice Boys field cannons would be used. Instead they would revert to using smaller cannon, which they would fire at the base of Walker's Pillar and at other parts of the City, including the four principal gates.

A HISTORY OF THE SHUTTING OF THE GATES CELEBRATIONS 1775–1985

Due to the heavy downpour of rain at midnight on 17th December 1893, the traditional firing of small cannon did not happen. This was the start of sporadic cannon absence as part of the 18th Celebrations. Small cannon would again be used in 1897, 1904 (after the burning of Lundy), 1910, 1913 and again in 1919, 1924, and from 1927 to 1934. The reintroduction of firing of cannon at midnight to usher in the Big Day occurred in 1927, but this too was short-lived.

Both Bobby Jacksons relate an incident that occurred one 17th night in the mid-1930s. The large cannon (London Company with the English rose on the top) situated beside the flagpole where the Union Jack flew from at the bottom of Walker's Pillar, had been cleaned out, charged and prepared for firing come midnight by the Finlay brothers. Bobby Jackson Senior along with Bobby Junior met up with the Finlay brothers in WG's Pub in Society Street for a few drinks in celebration of the coming occasion. As midnight approached this merry bunch made their way to the base of the Pillar, entrance was gained and Bobby Jackson Senior was given the privilege of firing the cannon. He declined, and instead gave Bobby Junior the privilege of firing it, which he did. Bobby Jackson Senior related what happened. He said,

> "He touched the firing hole with a taper and the next thing he remembered was seeing a flame about eighteen feet long fire out from the cannon's barrel followed by an enormous bang, which left Bobby Junior deaf for up to two months. He said that due to the force of the vibration of the gun being fired, he thought Walker's Pillar was going to fall down on top of him."

During and shortly after the Second World War (during Andy Creswell's time in making Lundy), thunder flashes were used to indicate that Lundy was about to be lit. The thunder flashes used were believed to be surplus leftovers from the local Home Guard.

It was approximately in the late 1940s or early 1950s that Mr Robert (Bobby) Jackson Senior suggested that the firing of cannon be reintroduced both at midnight to usher in Lundy Day and prior to the burning of the Lundy effigy.

The General Committee of the Apprentice Boys of Derry handed two small brass cannons over to Bobby Jackson. Each was approximately eighteen inches long and about four inches in diameter at the touch-hole end of the gun barrel, tapering to two and a half inches diameter at the other end of the gun barrel. Both cannons were mounted on a solid rectangular wooden block approximately sixteen inches long and about eight inches wide, painted black. When fully charged, the report from them was the equal to the sound of a twenty-four-pound field gun being fired. Mr Bobby Jackson Senior and Bobby Jackson Junior personally loaded these guns for firing and they were always loaded in Lundy's Room. It was a simple procedure. First, each cannon was loaded with an egg cup measure of gun powder, followed by stuffing some dry newspaper down the barrel, which is what made the loud bang as it left the gun barrel. Having put the paper into the barrel, it was then beaten down into place using a wooded pole and a hammer. The touch hole (firing point) was then primed and made ready for firing.

In relation to firing the cannon, health and safety was always a major concern for Bobby Senior and strict instructions were always followed. Each cannon was taken up onto the walls a short distance from the Apprentice Boys Memorial Hall to about the fourth tree. The cannon was placed on the ground and Bobby always instructed the one who had the honour of firing the cannon to stand behind the tree to prevent injury occurring, and then guided the individual to the touch hole with the lit firing stick. At no stage was anyone permitted to stand behind the cannon to fire, as it did recoil when fired. In the early 1960s thirteen shots were fired in honour of the Brave Thirteen who closed the gates of the City against the approaching forces of King James, but due to the early Troubles it was decided that a running fire of one plus three, equal to the number thirteen would be sufficient.

When the Apprentice Boys were prevented from firing their cannon on the City walls in the troublesome 1980s, they fired their cannon at the bottom of the steps leading to the walls with the barrel of the cannon facing down toward Butcher Gate. The police authorities would only permit them to fire one single shot.

Both brass cannons were kept under lock and key in a large green wooden box, better known as Lundy's box. The box itself was placed in Lundy's Room in the Apprentice Boys Memorial Hall and the only persons who had keys to this box were the General Secretary of the Apprentice Boys Association and Mr Bobby Jackson Senior. A third small cannon, which had its own small box belonging to the Browning Club, was also placed in this box. This Browning cannon was a small cartridge-firing two wheeled cannon, and when fired it sounded more like a shotgun firing than a cannon. This Browning Club cannon was fired only on a few occasions from the top of Walker's Pillar on the 17th night.

During Bobby Jackson's time, there was only one year when the brass cannons were not fired and that was in 1957. The then General Secretary of the Association, Mr A P Thompson, took it upon himself to remove the two cannons from Lundy's Room and lock them in the General Secretary's

Office, indicating that he had the authority to state whether or not they should be fired. When Bobby Jackson Senior went over to Lundy's Room to load the two brass cannons for firing, he was denied access to them by the General Secretary, who stated that they were the property of the General Committee and that he was acting on their behalf. Brother Thompson experienced the wrath of the Association by his actions, and the General Committee ensured that such behaviour would never again happen again.

This was not to be the last time that the General Committee would get itself into trouble. In 1969, a Government Ban was placed on the 18th Celebrations in the City. The Apprentice Boys General Committee held a secret meeting with the head of police in the General Committee Room in the Apprentice Boys Memorial Hall to see if some kind of deal could be struck, which resulted in a no deal situation. The General Committee on this occasion made a conscious decision to discourage outside Brethren from travelling to the City for Lundy's Day as they themselves had accepted the Ban placed on them, preventing them from parading in the City and from burning Lundy. This Ban also included the firing of the traditional cannon at midnight. Mr Bobby Jackson Senior took one of the brass cannons from Lundy's Room to his home in 3 Clarence Place, off Fountain Street. He loaded the cannon in the usual manner and fired it at midnight in Jimmy Logue's Builder's Yard, Fountain Street, which was adjacent to his own back yard. This brass cannon was later returned by Bobby to its rightful place in Lundy's Room, when it was safe to do so.

December 1981 was to be the last year that Mr Bobby Jackson Senior would fire one of his two brass cannons. As midnight approached, Bobby loaded the cannon in the usual manner. All the normal safety precautions were taken, but as soon as the lighted Roman candle touched the firing point, the cannon exploded. The Lieutenant Governor of the Association, Mr Stewart Heatley sustained lacerations to the abdomen and leg, and Master Ralph Sheppard received injuries to his leg and ankle. Both were admitted to Altnagelvin Hospital and were discharged the following morning. The police took away the remains of the cannon and the other intact cannon for examination and discovered that the two alleged brass cannons were in fact iron, with a covering of brass. The cause for the explosion, was a crack inside the iron barrel, and was not, as has been recently suggested, caused by using damp newspaper!

Despite reassurance from the police that it was not his fault, Mr Bobby Jackson Senior never recovered from the incident and never again fired any cannon to usher in the Big Day.

From this point onward a new cartridge firing cannon was used but it was no louder than a shotgun firing. A few years later a larger and much louder cannon was used to usher in Lundy's Day.

CHAPTER 5
MORE LUNDY'S

Londonderry was not the only place where the 18th was celebrated. In 1870-71 the construction and burning of Lundy effigies in various parts of Ulster was a reactionary act of defiance over how the Apprentice Boys of Derry Association was treated in Londonderry by both the civil and military authorities. What followed was that a number of principal cities and towns celebrated Lundy's Day by parading and burning their own effigy of the Siege traitor. This is by no means a comprehensive list, but it does highlight the political importance of the 18th Celebrations to the Protestant community in Ulster and the sheer determination to resist any attempt imposed by the Government to curtail religious liberty.

Belfast: The first Lundy to be burned in Belfast was in 1870 by Orangemen from the Derby Orange and Protestant Memorial Hall. On this occasion the Orangemen reacted against some legislative bills that had been posted around the City prohibiting any act in sympathy with the Derry Celebrations. The Orangemen viewed this as offensive, and with six drums and fifes they formed a procession in the Hall headed by a number of torch light bearers. Two men followed carrying a large bill, which proclaimed:

'Henceforth we are the Apprentice Boys.' The parade made its way outside the building and marched around the Hall enclosure three times, before forming a circle around their Lundy effigy, where Brother Criglington applied the match to it. Outside the enclosure of the Hall a massive crowd had gathered to support the Orangemen in an act of defiance to the local authorities. The effigy was reported to be the most grotesque figure ever seen. He had two faces and wore an old Repeal hat in deep mourning. The shoes were placed on the wrong feet and the calves of the legs were on the shins, but at least the effigy had a bundle of sticks on its back! As the proceedings concluded, Brother Criglington telegrammed Brother John Guy Ferguson, Corporation Hall, Derry, stating that: *"Lundy was successfully burned tonight at the Orange Hall, Agnes Street, Belfast, amid great enthusiasm."* Despite the large police presence, they did not interfere with the Celebration and no arrests were made.

In 1872, Belfast would again burn an effigy of Lundy on some old waste ground adjoining the School House, from a tree in Agnes Street. The figure was of large proportion and was made by two members of the newly formed Belfast Crimson Defenders Club. The effigy followed a similar pattern in dress to that of the Derry one. Lundy was clad in a suit of black, wore a general's hat, was stuffed with crackers and explosive materials, and burned for approximately for three quarters of an hour. In 1873, the location of burning Lundy had shifted from the old tree in the waste ground facing Agnes Street Orange Hall to being suspended from a large pole thrust out of one of the top floor windows, where it hung all day until its burning at six o'clock in the evening. The year 1876 is the next account of a Belfast burning of a Lundy, only this time the event is located the district of Club Row Ballymacarett. A large crowd waded through ankle-deep mud to witness the burning of a well-formed effigy.

It would be 1909 before the Apprentice Boys in Belfast would celebrate their next 18th December event. The usual trapping of the burning of Lundy was a distant memory and the event was celebrated by a combined loyal orders church service, organised to be held on a Sunday by the Apprentice Boys of Derry Clubs. The first event was held in Ulster Hall and was supported by the Royal Black Preceptory and several Belfast Orange Lodges. The parade formed up at the Clifton Street Orange and paraded to the Ulster Hall, where the Reverend R Ussher Green and the Reverend Alexander Gallaher conducted the Divine Service. A similar event was held two years later in 1911, only this time the Divine Service was conducted in Westbourne Presbyterian Church on a Sunday afternoon, supported by Apprentice Boys, the Black Institutions and the Orange Order members. The preacher was the Reverend William Witherow. In 1922 a further Church Service was organised to honour the memorial of the Brave Thirteen who closed the gates of Derry against King James II approaching forces. The service was conducted in St Jude's Church, Ballynafeigh, Belfast. The Reverend Louis W Crooks MA, and the Reverend J S Taylor conducted the service. A collection was taken up for the Lord Enniskillen Memorial Orphan Fund at each service. In 1938, Belfast held its last church service to commemorate the Shutting of the Gates. The Reverend Doctor Little conducted the service in Townsend Street Presbyterian Church on a Sunday afternoon, which was attended by all of the Loyal Orders in Belfast. A collection was taken up for the Lord Enniskillen Memorial Orphan Fund at each service.

In 1956, the Browning Parent Club presented a twelve-foot-tall effigy of Lundy, made by the Jackson family in the Derry tradition, to Bloomfield Browning Club and Belfast Branches of the Apprentice Boys Association. The Effigy was burned on waste ground at a railway embankment in Dee

Street. The Lieutenant Governor of the Apprentice Boys of Derry, Brother Dr W R Abernethy was given the honour of setting Lundy alight, much to the delight of the large gathered crowd.

The last Londonderry recorded burning of Lundy in Belfast was in 1970 in Dee Street and was organised by some of the Belfast Apprentice Boys of Derry Clubs and the Ulster Protestant Volunteers.

Coleraine: It was 1870 when the town of Coleraine burned its first recorded Lundy from one of the sycamore trees in Christ Church churchyard, which hung over into Church Street. By 1872, their effigy resembled that of the one burned in the Maiden City. It too was large in proportion, dressed in a black uniform which covered a wired frame. It had a bunch of large keys in one hand and a bundle of faggots attached to its back. Two Lundy effigies were burned in Coleraine in 1872. The first in the usual location on Church Street and a second Lundy was burned in 1872 near Church's Wall near the Railway Station. Lundy's effigy continued to be burned in Coleraine right up to 1879 and then a gap appeared until the Siege Centenary in 1888 where an effigy was burned in celebration of this significant event. But this was not without trouble. The Orangemen of Coleraine and District formed up with a colossal figure of Lundy in Northbrook Street and commenced to parade, but the police under the direction of the District Inspector of Law and Head Constable Tilson, interfered and prevented the effigy from being burned. However, the Orangemen had other plans, and despite the police interference they burned Lundy from a tree overhanging the road. No arrests were made and when Lundy had burned out, his remains were placed in a coffin and taken to the bridge and thrown into the River Bann. 1932 is the next year, recorded by the *Londonderry Sentinel*, of a Lundy being burned in Coleraine. This event was organised by the Killowen Branch of the Apprentice Boys of Derry, who conveyed a huge effigy of Lundy around the town in a horse-drawn van, followed by several Lambegs and fife and drum bands. The place of burning was at Victoria Park in the presence of a large crowd. This was the last recorded event of burning of Lundy in Coleraine by a Londonderry newspaper.

Strabane: The Orangemen of Strabane in 1882 decided that, in the spirit of the Siege defenders of Derry, they too should celebrate the Shutting of the Gates by burning an effigy of Lundy in the town. Shortly after midnight on Sunday, there were reports of a small cannon being fired from various parts of the town, which continued up until five o'clock in the morning. Finding a suitable location for burning of the Lundy proved somewhat difficult. Various sites had been looked at and it was finally decided that the effigy could be burned from an old poplar tree in the old burial grounds next to the wall connected to the church. The Lundy itself had all of the traits of the Derry one, accompanied by a brilliant fireworks display. The last mention of Lundy being burned in Strabane was in 1883.

Newtownlimavady/Limavady: 1870 is the first official record of a burning of Lundy in the town of Newtownlimavady. The fifteen-foot effigy was first paraded around the town on two poles, accompanied by the bands of Newtownlimavady and Edenmore Orange Lodge. The parade halted on Catherine Street, where a large pole had been erected and it was from there that Lundy was burned, lasting two hours. The location of the burning of Lundy moved in 1871 to the top of Main Street, but reverted again to Catherine Street from 1872 to 1875. Again, as in other location in Northern Ireland with the burning of Lundy, a gap of five years emerges and it is recorded that it was revived by some juveniles in Limavady in 1880, opposite the local police station in Catherine Street. Loyal Orange Lodge Numbers 255 and 657 were responsible for the organising and burning of Lundy in Catherine Street in 1886. The parade was led by Limavady No Surrender and Ballykelly flute bands, accompanied by a large crowd who paraded through the streets of Limavady, returning to Catherine Street to witness the burning of Lundy at seven o'clock in the evening.

A new added attraction to the 18th Celebration in Limavady occurred in 1898, under the auspices of LOL No. 657. This Lodge originally owned two ancient cannons (paid for by local subscription) but due to unknown circumstances, one of them ended up in Barley Park. On the death of Mr Ross, a leading Orangeman, the Park was sold and both young and old Orangemen raised the money needed to transport the cannon back to the Orange Hall to join its sister cannon, refurbish both gun carriages and place them at the front of the Orange Hall in preparation for the Big Day. When Lundy's Day finally arrived, the usual burning of the effigy took place in the usual location and the day's events concluded with the firing of the two cannon, a salvo of thirteen shots, in honour of the Brave Thirteen Apprentice Boys of Derry. By 1906, Limavady Apprentice Boys of Derry Club organised Lundy's Day with all the usual celebratory trimmings. The last mention of the two cannons being fired as part of Limavady's 18th Celebration was in 1948. Lundy's effigy followed the same design as that of Londonderry. The effigy stood sixteen feet and was about five feet across his shoulders. The basic effigy consisted of brown sacking which was stuffed with straw and was attached to an iron backbone. Its uniform was made of black sacking upon which the usual yellow stripes were painted. There were two white bills: the one on the front which was painted, 'Lundy

The Traitor' and the one on the back which had the words, 'The End Of All Traitors'. Lundy's face consisted of a tin face which was then covered in papier mâché to pick out the features of the face. The usual moustache was black chair stuffing glued on and this Lundy had a small bundle of sticks attached to his back. One major difference was noticeable about the Limavady effigy to that of Londonderry City: the effigy had no chicken wire to hold the whole structure together, so that when the match was applied, it soon dropped down onto the street below. This basic structure continued to be used well into the early 1980s, after which brown and black sacking was replaced by plastic bagging.

In 1967, the Limavady Apprentice Boys of Derry made a conscious decision to cancel the usual 18th Celebration in the town due to the outbreak of foot and mouth disease. This was a first since its inception in 1870, and was soon followed with another cancellation in 1970. The situation that led to the latter cancellation had its origins in Londonderry. The Government issued a Ban which prevented the Parent Clubs of the Apprentice Boys of Derry Association from conducting their annual 18th Parade to the Cathedral and from burning Lundy's effigy from Walker's Pillar on Derry walls. This proved to be an issue for the General Committee of the Apprentice Boys Association, as the Jacksons had already made a normal size (18 feet) effigy of Lundy for Walker's Pillar. As the Apprentice Boys in Limavady had already accepted the General Committee ruling and the Government's decision, some of the more loyal brethren, aided by Limavady and Londonderry Ulster Protestant Volunteers, approached the Jackson family to make a smaller Lundy (approximately fifteen feet by four feet across the chest) to be burned by them on the 18th night by the old Railway/Bus Station. After some discussion between the Jackson family, the UPV and the Apprentice Boys General Committee members, it was decided to swap the two Lundy's over. The Authorities in Londonderry permitted the Apprentice Boys to burn their Lundy in the car park facing the Memorial Hall, but were unaware that a swap had taken place. The Derry Lundy was placed on the back of a large lorry under the cover of darkness, and covered with a large green tarpaulin, although his feet could be clearly seen, and was driven to Limavady to await the big day. The smaller Lundy in Bobby's shed was also loaded onto a smaller lorry and driven over to the Apprentice Memorial Hall and placed in Lundy's Room. When the 18th arrived in Limavady, the Derry Lundy was hoisted up on the original pole used for burning Lundy, erected at the bus station, and a lorry decked in Ulster flags and Union Jacks was parked near Lundy's effigy. The Reverend Ian Paisley and other leading Ulster Protestant Volunteer members, along with some other members of the Apprentice Boys, including Bobby Jackson Senior addressed the gathered crowd. After the speeches were over, Lundy was set alight, the crowd cheered and the bands played appropriate loyal music. The event passed off peacefully and the police at no time made any attempt to stop the burning of Lundy from taking place.

Second to Londonderry, Limavady remained constant in keeping the tradition of the Shutting of the Gates alive, from its inception to this present day.

Lisburn: Lisburn burned its first Lundy in 1870, an event that was instigated by the local Orangemen in protest at the behaviour of the Government towards the Apprentice Boys of Derry Association in Londonderry. The Orangemen marched from all directions and assembled at the Market Square and then processed to the Protestant Hall in Railway Street. From this same Hall a life-size effigy of Lundy appeared, dressed in a black suit, three cornered hat and some very large boots. It was fixed to two poles and paraded through the principal streets of the town, returning to an elevated area near the Railway Station, better known as Lundy's Hill. There it was set alight much to the delight of the crowd, and when Lundy had burned out the various Orange Lodges made their way back to their respective Halls. The event was peaceful and no arrests were made. The year 1876 is the last record by a Londonderry newspaper of Lundy being burned in Lisburn. However, in 1972 the Lisburn Branch of the Apprentice Boys of Derry No Surrender Club, aided by the Reverend Ian Paisley and his followers, accompanied by two bands, walked from the Orange Hall in Railway Street to Bridge Street car park, where an effigy of Lundy was lit by the Reverend Ian Paisley. This was the final time Lundy was burned in Lisburn.

Omagh: In 1871, Omagh burned several effigies of Lundy at various parts of the town. The Resident Magistrate, forgetting that the Emblem Act was not now in force, wanted all flags removed from the Protestant Hall, but the Secretary refused and kept them flying until sunset. In the evening the Orangemen from various Districts dined together in honour of the day. Like other towns in Northern Ireland, the initial burning of Lundy effigies was clearly a protest to civil authorities, who were determined to stamp out the activities of the Apprentice Boys of Derry Celebrations in Omagh. As a large number of military men and police men had been drafted to Londonderry for the 18th Celebration from other towns in Ireland (this was pre 1922), it provided an opportunity for other sympathetic brethren to burn their own Lundy in defiance of civil authorities and the Government. The Orangemen in Omagh (according to local Londonderry newspapers) burned their second Lundy in 1884. This Celebration was organised by members of Lodge No. 850 and the location for the burning of Lundy was in Campsie. This event passed off without incident. In 1885 a nine-foot Lundy was burned from a tree in Campsie, or as it is called now, Sandy Row. Music was provided by the Omagh True Blues Flute Band. Orange Lodge No. 11 was responsible for the making and burning of Lundy in 1926. The life size effigy was placed on a cart and was paraded through the town to Campise, where it was suspended from a gallows and burned. On its chest was a placard which said, 'Let Traitors Beware'. Brother Robert Rodger, President of Omagh No Surrender Apprentice Boys of Derry Club, assisted by Brother Andy Cresswell, Brother William Duncan and Brother Lowery Nixon, constructed the Lundy effigy in the Orange Hall and, as in previous years, it was pushed in a hand cart to its place of burning. The last recorded account of Lundy being burned in Omagh was in 1950. Apprentice Boys clubs from Omagh, Cappagh, and Plumbridge paraded through the town, followed by burning a seventeen-foot effigy of Lundy. Mullaghmore and LOL No. 937 pipe bands provided the music on this occasion.

Donemana: Donemana No Surrender Apprentice Boys of Derry Club burned its first Lundy in 1906 from a scaffold loaned by Brother Adam Dunne outside the Orange Hall, following the pattern of the Derry one. Prior to the burning, the Donemana No Surrender Band led a procession of a thousand people through the streets of the town, returning back to the Orange Hall, where Lundy was set on fire. District Inspector Holmes and twenty police officers were on duty, but their services were not needed. By 1929, the Forbes family from Donemana were key players in building the Lundy effigy, forming Donemana Pipe Band and becoming leading members of the Donemana Apprentice Boys of Derry Murray Club. The location of the burning of Lundy had now changed from being outside the Orange Hall and was located at the old ruined castle on 'the Hill' until 1949. The framework for the Lundy effigy was made of metal, almost a skeleton kind of structure, in which straw was pushed in through the metal frame using old cut brush shafts. Lundy's uniform was pulled over this framework and the finishing touches applied. The face and hat were often made by Mr Bobby Jackson Senior of 3 Clarence Place, Londonderry. Lundy's proportion was quite large in comparison to other effigies made. He was sixteen feet in height, over five feet in width and weighed about half a ton. One of the main reasons the burning of Lundy came to a halt in Donemana was a sharp disagreement between some prominent members of the local Murray Club. In 1949, Bobby Jackson was approached to see if he could build a Lundy for the Donemana Club for burning on the 18th night. The Jackson family agreed and handed the large effigy, which had been made in Bobby's shed, to the local Apprentice Boys, and it was transported on the back of a lorry to Donemana Orange Hall. When the 18th arrived, Lundy was paraded through the small town towards the old castle on the hill, in torchlight. It was hoisted up but, before Bobby could made his usual speech in handing over the stick to light Lundy, several people charged with their torches to the effigy and set Lundy alight. In recognition of their hard work, Bobby was presented with an inscribed walking cane and Bobby's wife, Lily, was presented with an electric clock. The *Londonderry Sentinel* makes no mention of any further burning of Lundy after 1949, but there's mention in the Jackson archives that Bobby Jackson Senior supplied a hat and face, two lettered Bills, epaulettes and buttons, in 1955. The cost for supplying these items amounted to £5/10s, which was paid by the Donemana Apprentice Boys of Derry Murray Club.

Other Locations:

St Johnston, Donegal: The burning of a Lundy in the town of St Johnston, Donegal is first mentioned in 1875 and again in 1889. In 1899 an eight-foot-high Lundy was suspended from an ash tree in a field adjusted to the property of Mr James M'Kean on the edge of the town. The event was organised by St Johnston Flute Band and the occasion passed off peacefully.

Ballymacarett, Belfast, burned their first Lundy at a place known as Club Row in 1871.

The City of Armagh witnessed its first Lundy burning along with Portadown in the 1872. The Lundy in Portadown was burned at a place called Quarry Turn.

Lundy effigies were also burned in Enniskillen, Bushmills, Portrush, Portstewart, Ardstraw, Bready, Garvagh and Banbridge. The burning of Lundy in all of the mentioned towns was sporadic and short lived, except in Banbridge, which continues to burn their Lundy on top of the Bridge over the main street after the Relief of Derry Celebrations in August. Like the Lundy in Londonderry, the late Brother David McCormick's family was responsible for making this effigy, a tradition that is still carried on by his grandson Brother David Minnis. The responsibility for ensuring that this event continues to be celebrated is carried by Banbridge Apprentice Boys of Derry Club.

During the Great War of 1914-18, an effigy of Lundy was burned in the village of Gorenflos on 18th December 1916. This Celebration was organised by some soldiers from the 10th Battalion Royal Inniskilling Fusiliers, better known as the 'Derrys'. Mr Jim Donaghy from the Derrys states that:

> "An eight-foot effigy of the traditional pattern had been made by Sergeant Bomber Dan Gillen who was in charge of the bomber section. It hung from a beech tree in the centre of the village, opposite a big crucifix. We had the Battalion band; kegs of beer and a great party was in full swing when Gillen produced a bomb from a jam tin filled with gun powder. He had decided that this year we wouldn't burn Lundy – we'd blow him up! We eventually talked him out of his plan but during the burning ceremony he lit the bomb and threw it into the pond in the centre of the village. Well – it went off – and blew most of the windows in. He wasn't too popular and we had to pay for the damage."[16]

As well as the Lundy effigy on Walker's Pillar, Londonderry, Lundy effigies were burnt in other parts of the City, namely Fountain Street. In 1928, Mr Bobby Jackson Senior built a Lundy on behalf of the Maiden City Flute Band. This was built in the living room of his own home. Bobby said that his children should eat their tea from their Lundy table! When the Big Day arrived, Bobby, along with helpers, were unable to get the Lundy effigy out through the front door and so Mr Joe Revees removed the front window of Bobby's dwelling to lift Lundy out of the front room and into the street. Once this had been accomplished, the Lundy was suspended from a rope and pulley across Fountain Street near the junction of Hawkin

---

16   Mitchell, Gardiner. S. *Three Cheers for the Derry's* (2008) p 52

Street and Lower Fountain. As the Lundy was being hoisted into position on the 18th morning the rope snapped, the Lundy fell, and the pulley on which Lundy was suspended from hit Bobby Jackson on the head. Given the nature of the injury he was taken to the hospital where he received several stitches. While Bobby was at the hospital, the Finlay brothers put a bag of gunpowder in the Lundy, who was still lying on the ground on his back. When Bobby got back to the Fountain, the Lundy effigy was suspended from a large cast iron street lamppost just outside the house of Mrs Doherty, the other end of the rope being attached to one of the legs of her metal bed, which almost pulled her bed out of her bedroom window. Finally, it was suggested by Mr Harry McClay (Second Officer in the Fire Brigade) that instead of tying the end of the rope holding Lundy up to Mrs Doherty's bed, a large plank should be placed across the brace inside of the bedroom window. This they did and Lundy was successfully hoisted up into place and at seven o'clock on the 18th night, Lundy was set alight. As the bands played and the flames leaped up around Lundy, the bag of gunpowder exploded, smashing several windows, including Mr Kelly's large pub window. Bobby paid for and replaced them all. This was the first Lundy that the Jackson family made and it was the only occasion that the Maiden City Flute Band would be responsible for burning a Lundy in the Fountain.

In 1971, a small Lundy was burned outside some derelict houses facing Kennedy Street in Wapping Lane, just off Fountain Street. This Lundy was made under the direction of Bobby Jackson Senior by his grandson, Albert, which was his first attempt in following the Jackson family Lundy building tradition. Bobby's grandson made his second Lundy in 1972 which was suspended on the gable wall of the Paradise Pub, at the corner of Albert Place in the upper part of the Fountain.

CHAPTER 6
LESSER KNOWN FACTS ABOUT THE EIGHTEENTH DECEMBER CELEBRATIONS

Walker's Sashes

The first mention of the statue of Reverend George Walker on top of Walker's Pillar wearing a crimson sash was in 1935. This sash was made by Mr Bobby Jackson Senior. It was made from heavy rexine, seven foot in length, with an inch and a half white band around its border. There was a frill at the shoulder part of the sash and it was tied in three different places to keep it in place on the statue. Bobby Jackson Junior was always given the task of putting the sash on Walker. To achieve this, Bobby had to climb up on a conical convex fluted dome base measuring some three to four feet in height. The first tie was around the neck of the statue, the second underneath Walker's pointing arm and the last tie was around the bottom of the metal sword attached to Walker's left side. It was not a task for the faint hearted and on windy days the task more difficult to achieve. The first recorded graffiti on the sash was in August 1957. Lots more were added after, although some are now difficult to read. This crimson sash was only draped over Walker's statue for the two Apprentice Boys of Derry Celebrations. A separate sash was used for the Battle of the Boyne Celebration. This orange sash measured five feet ten inches long and was edged with a two-inch purple band around its edge and was tied in the same places as the crimson one. These two sashes currently remain in the Jackson family private collection.

The Shutting of The Gates Ceremonial Tradition

Even though the original four Siege gates had been altered or completely rebuilt – Bishop Gate 1788-89, Shipquay Gate 1805-08, Butcher Gate 1805-08 and Ferryquay in 1865 – all of them still had gates hung on them. From 1788, the Shutting of the Gates was part of the annual December Celebration. Reverend John Graham describes what took place in that year:

> "At two o'clock the forty-sixth Regiment and the Volunteers Corps paraded. The Apprentice Boys Company, commanded by Captain Bennet, went through the ceremonial of the shutting of the gates, supported by the Regulars and Volunteers in columns." [17]

In 1847, Robert Simpson in his book *The Annals of Derry* recalls the old gates were completely renewed when he was a little boy (this would fit in with the last recorded date of the actual Shutting of the Gates in

---

17   19 Graham, John. *Derriana* p 151

1814). The old gate irons were in the procession of the Apprentice Boys of Derry Association and stand ten feet five inches tall, the length of each gate varied according to the width of each new gateway. The thickness of the gates was six inches; one hinge was fixed at the top of the gate, and the bottom of the gate iron was slotted into an iron fixture fitted in the ground. The top hinge was fixed to each gate by nine bolts. Oak planking that made up each gate was placed horizontally and fixed into place by metal bolts which went right through each plank.

The *Londonderry Journal* in December 1804, 1805 and 1807 mention that part of the Celebration included the Londonderry Infantry parading to the four gates of the City, which they shut and fired over. The historian John Hempton also records that the Londonderry "*Yeomanry proceeded to the annual custom of Shutting the Gates and firing over them,*"[18] in 1813 and again in 1814. The Londonderry Sentinel records that in 1843 after the Apprentice Boys had fired their cannon at Artillery Bastion, the ceremonial of the shutting of the gates took place. (1843 is the last account of the actual gates being used as part of the December Celebration.)

In 1823, with three sets of the old gates gone, that part of the ceremony was replaced by musket fire combined with small cannon salvos. The small cannon used on this occasion was owned and fired by the Apprentice Boys of Derry Club. This part of the proceedings was maintained up to 1843, where they were joined by several other Apprentice Boys Clubs each with their own cannon and instead of firing their salvos at the gate entrance, they now fired them on top of each of the four principal gates. By 1866, the Apprentice Boys Clubs had confined their cannon fire to the Royal Bastion and the Mall Wall. The inclusion of the principal four gates, as a

---

18   Hempton, John. *The Siege and History of Londonderry* (1861) p 443

major part of the Shutting of the Gates Celebration was now confined to the annals of history. The last set of gates to be removed was the Ferryquay, which remained untouched until 1865.

Marching to the four principal gates as part of the Shutting of the Gates Celebration was reintroduced in 1965 as part of the actual parade prior to attending the Divine Service in the Cathedral. While the intent was honourable, it was short lived and no mention is made after this date. It was not until the early 1970s that the practice of visiting the four gates after the firing of the cannon at midnight was introduced. The rationale behind such a practice was to revive the custom that had been established by their forefathers in 1788. After the ushering in of the 18th morning by cannon fire, several senior members of the General Committee of the Apprentice Boys and some other Apprentice Boys members would walk toward Butcher Gate, then to Shipquay, Ferryquay and lastly Bishop Gate. On each occasion they would touch the corner of each gateway, indicating symbolically that the gate was secure and that all was well, a reminder of the action and spirit of the Brave Thirteen of 1688. This practice still continues up to this day every 18th morning.

Lundy's Boots

Since the 19th century, Lundy's boots have always consisted of two parts. The first part is the upper boot, which consists of a flat wooden boot-shaped sole measuring four feet five inches long by two feet five inches wide at the widest part of the boot, narrowing down to approximately eleven inches wide at the heel part of the upper boot. The thickness of this part of the boot is a half inch. This upper part of the boot is attached to

LESSER KNOWN FACTS ABOUT THE EIGHTEENTH DECEMBER CELEBRATIONS

the wooden sole around its edge by small tacks and then the whole upper boot is painted using black gloss. The second part of the boot is the actual sole, which measures twenty-eight inches long by ten and a half inches wide, narrowing down at the heel to nine inches. The actual heel measures three inches thick. No fewer than 350 nails are arranged around the edge and middle of the sole and heel. The under part of the boot is painted like that of an actual boot, i.e. leather sole and heel, with the dividing part between the heel and sole painted black. The chief reason why so much attention is placed on the lower part of the boot, the sole, is so that it can be presented to the person who is given the honour of lighting Lundy that year as a reminder of the honour given to them. The person behind this concept was Mr Bobby Jackson Senior of the Apprentice Boys of Derry Browning Parent Club. The customary attachment of Lundy's soles to the upper boot did not occur until the 17th night, prior to the firing of the cannons to usher in the Big Day. This was the final act of getting Lundy ready to be taken out in the early hours on the 18th morning to be hoisted up on Walker's Pillar. The sole part of the boot was always removed prior to Lundy being lit, and given, along with the stick used to light Lundy, to the honoured guest. The second sole is usually given to the President of the Club who is responsible for arranging the Shutting of the Gates Celebration, and is a tradition that continues up to this present day

The first presented Lundy's sole was in December 1937. The recipient was Master Billy White, who was the Grandson of Mr James White, Secretary of the Belfast Branch of the Browning Club and Vice-Chairman of the Belfast Amalgamated Committee. The second boot that year was given to Miss Major, a visitor from Melbourne and a grand-niece of Mr J Allan Osborne, Milford, who took the sole back with her to Australia. Mr and Mrs E W Jones QC, MP for Londonderry and a member of the Browning Parent Club was the first to be given the honour of nailing on Lundy's soles in 1965, just prior to the Crimson Ball on the Friday evening.

The Traditional Burning of Chimneys

The *Londonderry Sentinel* in 1901 records that during the burning of Lundy on Walker's Pillar a number of residents in the Nailor's Row area of the Bogside set their chimneys alight, implying that it was their prescriptive right to do so. The dense smoke blew across the walls and the flames from some of the chimney pots were quite high. It is difficult to trace when this tradition first started. What the *Sentinel* does suggest is that this was a standard custom for the Bogside residents. Its purpose was twofold: firstly, to spoil the view of all who had gathered on the City walls to observe this long-standing tradition by polluting the area with thick black soot smog; secondly, for those living close to Walker's Pillar, lighting their chimneys shortly after Lundy had be lit and hoisted, meant no prosecution would follow as it would be difficult for the police to prove that the chimney fire was not started by a spark from the burning Lundy or from a rocket fired from the top of Walker's Pillar. The last record of the burning of the chimneys tradition is 1945, but this does not imply that it did not carry on before the redevelopment around the Walker's Pillar area in the early 1960s, as the last Lundy to be burned from the Pillar was 1968. During the making of Lundy, some people from Nailor's Row asked for shavings/straw to set to fire to, and asked and what time Lundy was going to be burned. This would mean that they could light their chimneys without being prosecuted for doing so. It was impossible to prove that it was not one of the sparks flying from the burning Lundy, that resulted in a chimney catching fire!

Change of Date for The Burning of Lundy

The Shutting of the Gates Celebration has always been observed on 18th December since its inception. There are several reasons for this. Primarily this event was locally celebrated by citizens in the City during the early part of the 19th century, and it was not until 1839 that people started to flock in from Tyrone and Donegal for the Celebration. The growth of the railway (the Londonderry to Coleraine and on to Belfast line opened in 1845) made what was a local tradition into one that was more accessible to all followers of the Apprentice Boys Association. The Londonderry to Enniskillen (later called the Great Northern) line also opened in 1845, whereas the Londonderry to Letterkenny railway (better known as the Lough Swilly) opened 1863. This new surge in travel and accessibility also led to the growth of the Apprentice Boys Association province-wide.

Mr William Johnstone MP of Ballykilbeg House, County Down, who had been invited to be a member of the Murray Parent Club in 1860, first mooted that the great story of the Maiden City should not be shut up in Londonderry, but proclaimed throughout the province of Ulster and that all true loyal Protestants should follow in the footsteps of the Brave Thirteen who closed the gates against a rebel force. This vision would become a reality due to public transport swelling the numbers of marchers and spectators alike into the City for the Two Big Days. The General Committee of the Apprentice Boys was formed on 22nd November 1859 and drew up its first Rule Book. Brother John Guy Ferguson was elected as the first Governor 1867. As Parent Clubs were established, a growing surge to establish other Apprentice Boys of Derry Clubs in various parts of Ulster and beyond began to emerge. The Scottish Amalgamated Committee of the Apprentice Boys of Derry emerged in 1946. Belfast and district followed suit in 1925, Ballymena and district in 1948, South Derry and East Tyrone 1954, South West Ulster 1963, Northwest in 1971 and County Down in 1948. These various Amalgamated Committees all had a chairman who had a seat at the General Committee Meetings chaired by the Governor of the Association. It was at the General Committee meetings that issues concerning the Association were debated and resolved. It was at one such meeting where the issue of celebrating 18th December during a week day was discussed. The reason for debating this subject was simple. Those who had jobs often found it difficult to book a day off work and would often lose a day's pay for taking time off, so the first burning of Lundy on a Saturday took place in 1970 and continues right up to this present day, even though this suggestion had been dismissed by the General Committee initially in 1959.

Payment for the Building of the Lundy Effigy

One of the earliest records of money being paid towards the cost of building Lundy's effigy was in 1829, where the sum of £2/10s and no pennies was paid out to build it. This was a considerable sum of money to pay out for the building of an effigy, which would not have been big, as it was suspended at the south-east side of the Corporation Hall in the Diamond. No doubt a huge chunk of this money would have been spent

LESSER KNOWN FACTS ABOUT THE EIGHTEENTH DECEMBER CELEBRATIONS

on buying the materials to build Lundy and the remaining few shillings given to the Lundy builders as a token of good will.

By 1862, the cost of building the effigy seems to have fallen on the Murray Club who was ordered to pay £1 towards the overall coast of making Lundy. One of the men responsible for helping to make the Lundy that year was Mr T Irvine of the Murray Club. A possible reason why the Murray Club was ordered to pay £1 towards the cost of building Lundy and not the rest of the Parent Clubs is that it was the Murray Club's responsibility for organising the 18th Celebration on that particular year.

Sharing the overall cost of building the Lundy effigy by all of the Apprentice Boys Parent Club became common practice due to an amendment to the Apprentice Boys Rules in 1962: *"That from December, 1961, each Parent Club shall be levied with one-eighth of the total cost of making the effigy of Lundy and providing power, rockets, etc."* How much that amounted to is not clear.

The overall cost paid to the Lundy builders in 1965 amounted to £12 and no pennies, and payment was always made to each helper on the 18th night. This was a practice that continued right up to 1985 when the Jackson family built their last effigy of Colonel Robert Lundy. Monies paid would not have sufficiently paid the builders for the number of hours given to constructing the effigy. But payment by the General Committee was welcomed as a token of goodwill and appreciation for the devotion given each year to ensuring that the Lundy burning tradition would always continue in the Maiden City.

Bands – The Browning Memorial Wreath

In 1959, the General Committee under the Governorship if Dr W R Abernethy believed that bands were not integral to the 18th Celebrations. It had been suggested by some of Apprentice Boys members, that maybe the Celebrations could take place in the evening which would permit employees, who were band members, to take part in the Celebrations without having to take a day off work and lose a day's pay for it. Or that the event was moved to the nearest Saturday and not on the actual 18th date. Both suggestions were dismissed by Abernethy who said that:

> "There were no bands when the Apprentice Boys closed the Gates in 1688. We commemorate the act, and bands are incidental. They are very welcome when they are able to come along, but people must get away from the idea that bands are essential to the anniversary."

Since 1817 when the Londonderry Yeomanry Drums and Fifes led the procession on the 18th Anniversary, 1959 was the first occasion when no bands took part in the Celebrations, and it would not be the last. Due to an outbreak of foot and mouth disease in 1967, the General Committee again under the Governorship of Dr W R Abernethy appealed to all Branch Clubs along with bands, that for health reasons they should not attend the Burning of Lundy Celebration. The local newspaper records that due to this precautionary measure the parade was small, but the Apprentices' enthusiasm remained resolute. The final dates for no recorded of bands being present for Lundy's Day was in 1969 when the Government place a ban on the event, and in 1970, where records of loyal band music was played from one of the top windows of the

Apprentice Boys Memorial Hall during the burning of Lundy in the car park in Society Street.

The only recorded wreath laying ceremony at the Browning Memorial plaque, facing the Guildhall took place in December 1966. The wreath was made up of holly and laurel and was placed at the plaque by the Governor of the Apprentice Boys Dr W R Abernethy.

The Crimson Ball

The first Crimson Ball to take place as part of the evening festivities was in 1865. It was a follow-on from the annual Soiree in the old Corporation Hall. The attendance was large and it proved to be a huge success. The music was provided by the Maiden City Band who performed from the gallery and the catering was carried out by Mr Johnston, cook and confectioner of Shipquay Street. In 1866 the Britannia Flute Band provided the music for the Ball. In 1870 the annual Soiree and Ball were cancelled due to the troubles around the 18th Celebrations. A lapse of six years occurred before the next Soiree and Crimson Ball would be held and the new location would be the Upper Hall in the Apprentice Boys Memorial Hall, Society Street, where it would permanently remain. But as ever, this evening event always happened on the actual 18th after the burning of Lundy, commencing at eight o'clock and finishing in the small hours of the following day. This tradition continued up to 1895 when the tea and Ball were replaced by a dinner. Mr Johnston of the Criterion provided the catering for this event. But even the 18th Dinner was soon replaced by a supper and entertainment. By 1807 the supper had gone and the Anniversary Social Meeting, which consisted of tea, speeches and some musical talent via song and recitations was in place. Like all of the previous events, this too was held at eight o'clock on the 18th night after the burning of Lundy, only on this occasion, the ladies of the Apprentices organised all of the catering. 1911 is the last recorded account of an 18th December Social.

The Browning Parent Club in 1919 held a very successful dance in the Memorial Hall on the Thursday evening after the burning of Lundy. The Britannia Brass and Reed Band provided the music along with a selection of various singers. Refreshments were provided by Fosters of the Strand Road. Almost thirty years later, in 1956, the Browning Parent Club revived the Crimson Ball. Unlike the former event, this was on a much grander scale with tickets costing 5s per head. Over six hundred people, along with civic dignitaries attended the evening. Dancing commenced after the Grand March at nine o'clock to two am the following morning. This Grand March consisted of one large Crimson flag being carried up the centre of the large hall on the top floor of the Memorial Hall, flanked on either side by two sword bearers. All wore black ties and crimson sashes. The tune played as the colour party processed up the centre of the Hall was *'Derry's Walls'* and the Crimson flag was handed over to the Governor of the Apprentice Boys of Derry Association. Having had a successful revival of the Crimson Ball, the Browning Parent Club continued to organise this evening event for the next eight years. The format remained the same, but with one exception: instead of the Crimson Ball being held on the evening of the burning of Lundy, it was moved in 1959 to the 17th night. At eleven o'clock the Grand March would take place in which members of the Browning Club along with their wives/partners would form up behind the Crimson flag party and march around the hall and up the centre, where the Crimson flag would be handed over to the

Grand procession at the Browning Club Crimson Ball on the 17th December 1959. The Governor of the Association, Dr. Abernethy receiving the crimson standard.

Governor. Once this part of the proceedings was over, the Governor along with interested parties would leave the hall at five minutes to midnight and make their way to the City walls for the firing of the cannons to usher in the Big Day. Dancing commenced after the firing for another hour or so. Mr Bobby Jackson Senior, Lundy builder and a member of the Browning Parent Club, introduced nailing the soles of Lundy's boots onto the effigy as part of the 17th Celebrations. This was final act in preparation for the morning's events. Before daylight Lundy would be carried out by dedicated members of the Apprentice Boys under the guidance of Bobby up onto the walls towards Walker's Pillar and hoisted up for all to see. The first honour of nailing on Lundy's soles prior to the Crimson Ball was given to the Brother R Chichester-Clarke MP for Londonderry City, and Brother E W Jones QC and MP for Londonderry City. The 17th night Crimson Ball was last traditional Ball organised by the Browning Parent Club in 1964, thereafter the event was less formal and the organisers from the Memorial Hall Social Committee introduced something which resembled more of a social evening.

Catholic Participation in The Shutting of The Gates Celebration

Since 1788 the Catholic clergy in the City took an active part in the procession and the jovial evening activities in the Town Hall. The prime mover in offering this invitation was the Lord Bishop Frederick Hervey Earl of Bristol. The Catholic Bishop for the City, Dr Philip McDevitt, encouraged Catholics to celebrate the Siege events, as an act of religious freedom for all. The Bishop's sentiments divided the Catholic community, and despite his best efforts to keep a spirit of harmony and mutual understanding, his work only lasted until his death in 1798. Dr Philip McDevitt was succeeded by Bishop Charles O'Donnell, who was equally zealous in trying to maintain a harmonious spirit between both communities. He was nicknamed 'Orange Charlie.' This was because of the political stand he took against the local Ribbon men and those who tried to stir up trouble in the aftermath of a huge Rally held in the City in support of Daniel O'Connell's Emancipation Bill. Not all Catholics were opposed to the Celebration of Siege events, many lined the streets to watch the pageantry unfold and to witness the burning of the Siege traitor, Lundy. Bishop Peter McLoughlin was consecrated to the See in Raphoe in 1802 and translated to the See in Derry in 1823. He too followed in the footsteps of his successor amid rapid changes in the political and demographics in the City. Like all of his successors, he too took part in the Siege Celebrations, but by 1837 a dramatic change took place and the Catholic clergy withdrew all association with Civic Siege Celebrations.

The harmony and political respect that once abided in celebration of religious freedom was now laid aside. A new political and sectarian mood emerged in pursuit of dominance and self-survival. However, there were still a few Catholics that would continue to enjoy the Two Big Days beyond the 1980s.

The Flags, Banner and Lights on Walker's Pillar

In 1829, once the statue of Reverend George Walker been elevated onto his plinth at the top of the Memorial Pillar, a large Crimson flag with the numerals 1688 in its centre was hoisted up on the flagpole beside him. The

This photo was taken in 1968 capturing the last Lundy to be burned on Walker's Pillar. The photo captures some of the crowd looking up at an British army helicopter hovering overhead.

The effigy of Lundy, the Traitor enveloped in flames.
50TLS25

The burning of Lundy in the car park facing the Apprentice Boys Memorial Hall on Saturday 22nd Dec 1970. This 15ft Lundy was made in Bobby Jacksons shed in Clarence place and was deemed for Limavady, but was switched for the 18ft Derry Lundy, when the General Committee of the Apprentice Boys discovered that Lundy was not going to be burned from Walker's Pillar.

First Lundy effigy hanging from New Gate, Saturday 15th December 1971.

Last burning of Lundy from New Gate 19th December 1973..

exception to this was in 1870-71, when the civil authorities refused the Apprentice Boys access to the Pillar to raise the Crimson flag over Walker's statue. From 1872 the Crimson flag, a symbol of Derry's unconquered City, was flown proudly beside Governor Walker's statue during the Apprentice Boys Celebrations and the Battle of the Boyne (the flag flown for the battle of the Boyne was orange with a six-inch border of purple) until 1973 when Walker's Pillar was destroyed by a bomb. However, Mr Bobby Jackson Senior and Mr Drew Porter made a new set of metal brackets and attached them to the right-hand side of Walker's plinth, facing Butcher Gate, where they then placed a large flagpole and hoisted a Crimson flag on it for the August and 18th Celebrations. This practice continued up until the site was cleared for building the new Walker's plinth in1992. The Union Jack was first flown at the Royal Bastion in 1898 along with the Royal Ensign, and both flags were hoisted at each side of the Bastion. The Union Jack was hoisted beside the cannon facing Butcher Gate and the Royal Ensign facing up towards the Double Bastion. Flying the Union Jack at the base of the Pillar would be a tradition that would continue right up to 1992. The flagpole from which it was flown measured eighteen feet long, approximately eight inches at the bottom and tapering at the top to four inches. It was surmounted by an eight-inch circular flat top through which the rope for hoisting up the flag was threaded. This flagpole was kept in Lundy's Room, which was the only place it could be stored, and provided easy access for getting it out for the big Celebrations.

This Union Jack at the Bottom of the Pillar had a second function. It was used to indicate to the gathered crowd when Lundy was about to be burned. Prior to Lundy being set on fire, the flag would be lowered, as it would have been sacrilege if it had of been set alight from a burning spark from Lundy!

LESSER KNOWN FACTS ABOUT THE EIGHTEENTH DECEMBER CELEBRATIONS

As in 1857 as part of the decoration at the top of the Pillar for the December Celebration, four Banners were attached to the railings commemorating the victories of 1688 to 1691. They had a crimson background with large yellow lettering: Derry, Aughrim, Enniskillen and the Boyne. They were last used in 1859. The Royal Standard was also raised for the first time for the December Celebration in the Double Bastion beside the Roaring Meg in 1840. This continued annually up to 1900.

It had been suggested that as part of the renovations to Walker's Pillar, the area should be floodlight on the 17th night prior to burning of Lundy the following day. So, in December 1968 at the cost of £5,000, the Governor of the Apprentice Boys of Derry, Dr Abernethy, switched on the floodlights, much to the delight of the gathered crowd. However, this new initiative was short-lived due to the outbreak of the Troubles in the City and the last time they were switched on was in December 1970. the Pillar was blown up in 1973.

Lundy Songs

In 1842 a song was published in the *Londonderry Sentinel*, which poked fun at the new reformed Corporation's approach to the burning of the Lundy effigy. The song was entitled:

SONG ON THE BURNING OF THE EFFIGY OF THE TRAITOR LUNDY IN DERRY, IN 1842.

Air – "Ballinamona Oro"

Suspended once more from the end of a rope,
The effigy grim of that friend to the Pope,
The false traitor Lundy has swung in the wind,
And perish'd in flames, though some Burgesses kind
In Council so gravely when seated,
His fate deeply commiserated,
And talked in tone quite elated
That burn'd he this year should not be.

The Hall, they declared, had become now their own,
Here laws they could make, abrogate, or postpone;
And, to their Wig Radical principles true,
The 'Prentice Boy spirit, they vow'd, they subdue;
And Lundy, whose name they respected,
From insult should hence be protected;
For him would no pole be erected
This year, on our Corporation Hall.

But early on the Monday the brave 'Prentice Boys
Hung up the vile image 'mid cannons' loud noise,
On Walker's high Pillar, the suitable place,
To publish once more the deceiver's disgrace;
While thousands assembled, delighted,

To see the traitor, ignite,
Who fealty to William had plighted,
But labour'd his cause to betray.
The glorious day which historians own
Establish'd in Britain a Protestant throne,
We still will in Derry each year celebrate,
While joy bells and cannon the triumph repeat,
Hurrah, then, for Brogan and Co. oh,
To Mass let the Jesuits go, oh,
But here we'll soon teach them to know, oh,
No Lundy's will Aldermen be.

A Poem on the Eighteenth of December 1869
The Anniversary of the Shutting of the Gates
Published Londonderry 1870

The Eighteenth of December is now passed away,
And many people thought that it would be a bloody day,
But fortunate it came to pass that it passed off so quiet,
No blood was shed, no angry words, nor an attempt at riot.
Horse and foot had poured in our city to protest,
The horse in prancing through the streets had powerful effect,
The forty-fourth and the seventeenth, from headquarters sent down,
To protect the quiet citizens of this old ancient town.
The Royal Irish C's were here, their equal never seen,
A splendid force, with harp and crown, clothed in dark green;

A HISTORY OF THE SHUTTING OF THE GATES CELEBRATIONS 1775–1985

Those troops were posted everywhere, the gates, the lanes, and streets,
The walls and Diamond manned by them no opposition meets,
Some came by train, some marched on foot, and others came on cars,
A martial train of armed men, those gallant sons of Mars;
They came prepared for battle, for fighting is their trade,
But no enemy appearing it turned out a grand parade.
Our city thus was garrisoned by some two thousand men,
The 'Prentice Boys for to protect for fear had come on them.
The Defence Association had nobly kept their word,
That they should dare for to turn out the Boys thought it absurd;
But out they came in thousands from many parts around,
With thorns black well-armed they thronged our ancient town,
Through gates and streets were seen those men, with steady, warlike pace,
Descendants of a noble stock, an old and ancient race.
The excitement greater now became, some fears did entertain
That collision would take place, but, thanks their fears were in vain;
What caused the great excitement that did this day prevail,
'Twas owning to processionists, who never yet did fail
To cause great animosity, and always create a noise,
The processions of a party they call Apprentice Boys,
Who sow the seeds of discord, thus causing mortal strife,
That often ends in bloodshed and danger unto life.
Those annual processions of late years have become
A disgrace to all humanity, a yearly social bane,
Insulting to all classes, and degrading to the mind,

LESSER KNOWN FACTS ABOUT THE EIGHTEENTH DECEMBER CELEBRATIONS

But the influx of low Orangemen, who twice yearly us invade
To disturb our peace and quiet, this motley ribald crew
Come here with bands and bannerets, their insults to renew;
With flags and orange sashes our town they inundate
To carry out their programme, and display their bitter hate;
But a wise determination our passion for to drown
Those displays of party triumph we can surely put them down,
An end will then be put to them, and Derry will be freed,
We here must live in harmony, for this all have agreed,
Those annual insults heaped on us made men at least agree,
Who did combine at the right time from such to set us free.
The working men of Derry, to their credit be it told,
Have taken steps in the right path, manly steps and bold,
They have found a society, with rules within the law
To guide them as a body in those rules there's not a flaw;
This temple great of harmony the working classes built,
With busts of love and charity this noble temple gilt,
They dug deep its wide foundation, they did those sons of toil,
And the acorn of friendship they have planted in our soil,
The seed soon germinated, it's now a mighty tree,
Its branches spanning counties round from Derry to the sea,
Intertwined with one another, its foliage ever green,
It's the largest tree in Derry, the largest ever seen.
I'll now to the processions and strive them to describe,
Their numbers, route, and bearing, nothing will I hide.
At early dawn the bells announced the commencement of the play,
And poor Lundy was suspended quite dead from where he lay,
The traitor greatly was fatigued and stood in want of rest,

A HISTORY OF THE SHUTTING OF THE GATES CELEBRATIONS 1775–1985

A march on the police was stole, the Boys thought it was best,
On Thursday night they hauled him up, placed at Walker's side,
And left him there to watch and guard the lord in whom they pride,
The winds blew high, the night was cold, no place his head to hide,
Poor Lundy had a heart's disease, he here sank down and died,
For this they him suspended from the pillar of their lord,
But his innocence was proved by the breaking of the cord.
In its proper place I'll it describe, his burning for the last time,
His funeral dirge how it was played, the breaking of the line.
The Apprentice Boys at ten o'clock assembled in the Hall,
Kilbeg was there, and Garvagh too, the Maddens, orange all;
Great Guy (not guy of Warwick) as Governor was proud
That he that day had chief command as leader of the crowd;
I missed the mourning emblems from the hat was on his head,
He should have worn crepe that day, his Mavis she was dead;
John Rea was there, the hero bold, M'Kenna did kick out,
Prepared to run if there was fun, or if there were a rout;
Blacker than Black Stewart was there, I did not see Lord Clod,
It's said he thought himself too high to mingle with the mob;
There were Templeton's and printers, and Davy sweet so grand,
But end was there with tuffy cart held ticket clerk by hand,
Distiller, Mormon, drummer, he's a credit to them all,
He supplied the Boys with codlin for their supper and their ball.
There were many more distinguished for their dress and out-ward show,
Pawnbrokers made a fortune the night before you know;
They took out their tugs on Friday on Tuesday put them in,

LESSER KNOWN FACTS ABOUT THE EIGHTEENTH DECEMBER CELEBRATIONS

The brokers solemnly declared their desks were filled with tin,
The speaking cheering, Kentish fire, the band and party tunes,
Took up some time when lo a line they saw approach their rooms,
One thousand men in bold array led by the daring Hugh,
The 'Prentice Boys now made less noise, they knew not what to do.
Those men led by M'Laughlin marched on up Bishop street,
It was but a contingent who their friends had come to meet,
M'Laughlin, he of Rossville street, M'Keown and Divin too,
Mr M'C and Halferty they had hard work to do.
The greatest praise is due to them for they did well command,
And carried out the noble work that they and others planned.
Contingents now came pouring in from every part around
That actually did frighten the people of the town,
But those men so well conducted were that under no pretence
Did they attempt in any way to give the least offence,
Their manly bold appearance all seemed for to admire,
Their eyes did flash as in they came with bold and martial fire,
They passed on in thousands strong to an appointed place,
Where a procession was formed soon of this young gallant race.
The Apprentice Boys now formed were, from the Hall came every man,
Men and boys in rows four deep in accordance with programme,
To Church they went as were their wont and heard a sermon long
From Mr Scott on loyalty, in language very strong.
He lashed the stumping orators, who run from place to place
Spouting their disloyalty, to their country a disgrace;
With a tongue of bitter eloquence, without dread or fear,
He lashed those hounds like spaniels, they'll never back come here.

A HISTORY OF THE SHUTTING OF THE GATES CELEBRATIONS 1775–1985

I'll now leave them and their sermon I hear the beat of drum,
It's the great and grand procession from Murray's yard they come,
In rows abreast, in four you see, how proudly they do march,
Not like the counter party who breakfasted on starch.
The workmen's band are leading them in strains of music sweet,
And strongly reinforced they are as they pass by each street.
The Stand is gained, one loud long cheer is heard for John Ahoo,
They now enter the Corn Market, it's their great rendezvous.
There's another great procession approaching nigh at hand,
Led by those steady valiant boys, the city's tradesmen's band;
Ha here comes the crowning climax, some say five thousand men,
With splendid flags that flauntingly are floating over them,
The gallant flutes in uniform, Derry's senior band,
Their music sweet discoursing are as they sweep down the Strand.
Arrived at their great rendezvous a procession grand is formed,
With virgin flags that's gaily trimmed, with mottoes well adorned;
Processionists now sally forth, about eight thousand strong,
The footpaths densely crowded are as they thus pass along.
In the advancement are stalwart men, yes men of Celtic race,
Determined men, if danger come they'll meet it in the face;
Three bands now sweetly playing are, flags waving high in the air,
On, on they marched until they pass'd the fountain in the Square,
There were band men six hundred in centre, front and rear,
They were silent and determined men in whom there was no fear;
The column still pressed forward the crowd becoming great,
They enter'd the Maiden City and passed through Shipquay Gate,
The noble house of Aushfield, sprung from the great Tyrconnel,
Was represented here this day by the famous John O'Donnell,

LESSER KNOWN FACTS ABOUT THE EIGHTEENTH DECEMBER CELEBRATIONS

He led the van (it was his place) unarmed with sword or lance,
Though heir unto his uncles who trod the soil of France,
Fighting England's battles as an O'Donnell Ahoo,
And helped to gain the victory of blood-stained Waterloo.
There's many more that should be named but want of space and time
Compels me not to mention them, or lengthen out this rhyme.
The procession pass Sir Robert, the Dimond, Bishop's Gate,
They reached the foot of Bishop Street where thousands them await,
They now turn to the new bridge and up through Ferry Street,
They tread their way the band they play our ancient airs so sweet,
The Diamond pass'd, down Butcher street they onward wend their way,
The gate when reached the band stuck up our own St. Patrick's Day;
Down the Cowbog they passed the Strand and up Gt. James Street,
Cheers from the crowd, both long and loud, here the procession great
They crossed the Moor, the rain down pour, the clouds look low and dark;
They enter by an open gate a large and spacious park,
The flagstaffs firmly planted are, the scene looks great and grand,
It's right opposite the pillar where Walker takes his stand.
The Apprentice Boys for the last time I see assembled here,
They look depressed and weary too, they something seem to fear.
Their procession was a failure it was so very small,
I've often seen some thousands more on such days on the Wall.

From gate to gate they countermarched, the same through every street,
No cheering met them on the way, no crowds came them to meet,
At every gate they gave three cheers, and caried out "No Surrender"
—
It's the last time they'll celebrate the eighteenth of December.
The walls perambulated were, no crowds did follow them,
Their guns crowds often did attract, they'll ne'er have them again.
Their crimson flags and bannerets they now can stow away,
When Dowse next time shall be returned we'll let them out that day,
For to celebrate his triumph all parties should unite,
And let our flags be blended, the crimson, green and white.
The hour now see is come at alas poor Lundy for to fire,
He is let down mist shouts and cheers and groans from their own crier,
The rope gives way, oh woe to us, the Boys cry out and wails,
As they see Lundy tumble down and fall within the rails;
Again hoisted up, oh ominous, it's an unlucky time,
Poor Lundy gets another fall by breaking of the line.
A new rope now the Boys procure, and Lundy with great ire
Is hauled up, the matched applied, and he is set on fire.
He badly burns, the evening wet, of him no more in verse,
He has burned out, they give three cheers, and quietly disperse.
On the Lone Moor, in that great park, twelve thousand people stand,
Men from counties round about, fair daughters of our land.
O'Donnell is now addressing them, in thrilling accents told

LESSER KNOWN FACTS ABOUT THE EIGHTEENTH DECEMBER CELEBRATIONS

How they had gained a victory more precious than gold.
His oration like a Phillipic upon the audience fell,
It came like an electric shock, and bound them like a spell –
He thanked his friends from coming from far-famed Inishowen,
From the counties of Fermanagh, Donegal, and sweet Tyrone,
The county Derry men he thanked from coming here that day,
And told them they would end the scene by burning Castlereagh;
This man had sold his country's rights, his friends and sacrificed,
And when he thought upon his crimes he cut his throat and died.
Cromwell, far worse than Castlereagh, his king he did behead,
The nation's rights he did usurp, and ruled in his stead,
He was a tyrant, murderer, his path a field of blood,
Three hundred souls in Drogheda were murdered at his word,
They there had fled for shelter, their cry for mercy spurned,
That is the reason we this day his effigy have burned.
Cromwell now Castlereagh suspended from on high
Wee fired at once the blaze and smoke ascending to the sky.
They burned bright, a pleasing sight, there were loud cheers and groans,
The scene now ends and all depart in quiet to their homes.
Good bye, my friends, I now have done, I know you'll say amen,
I hope something will soon turn up to exercise my pen.

List of people who had the privilege of setting fire to the effigy of Colonel Robert Lundy

The earliest record of named people who were given the privilege of setting light to the Lundy effigy starts in 1892.

> 1892: Master Arthur Alexander (grandson of Lord Bishop Alexander of Derry)
> 1894: Master Beresford
> 1895: Master John Holland (8 years old; he was later to become Governor of the Association)
> 1899: Master James Colhoun (eldest son of the Sentinel newspaper proprietor)
> 1900: Master William Colhoun (son of the Sentinel newspaper proprietor)
> 1901: Master Jack Cladwell (son of C S Cladwell solicitor)
> 1902: Miss Dolly Norrie (First female and daughter of the Lundy builder Dickie Norrie, who was also Caretaker of the Memorial Hall)
> 1903: Master Jack Colhoun (son of the Sentinel newspaper proprietor)
> 1904: Master Norrie (youngest son of Dickie)
> 1905: Master James Anderson (Dublin, and grandson of Mr James Wilton, Derry)
> 1906: Masters Wilton (sons of Mr James Wilton)
> 1908: Hon. Ezekiel Corry (son of the Earl of Belmore)
> 1909: Miss May Norrie (daughter of Dickie)

1910: Miss Molly Holland (4 years old, daughter of Mr and Mrs Thomas Holland)

1911: Master George Stacy Skipton (youngest son of Mr S Kennedy Skipton J P, Derry)

1913: Master Francis James Kellett (4 years old and son of Brother James Kellett)

1914: Master John Harland Ferguson (son of Brother John Ferguson President of the Browning Parent Club)

1915: Masters Magee (sons of Mr Gilbert Magee)

1916: Masters John Herbert Kerr and Robert Charles Lindsay

1918: Miss Inez Felicia Muriel Forbes and Master William George Gale Kellet (nephew of the General Secretary)

1920: Burned during the Troubles outside the Memorial Hall by one of the Lundy builders

1921: Mrs Tom McGregor and Miss Rachel Cresswell

1922: Sir Malcolm Macnaghten KC

1923: Miss Lizzie Smith and Miss Lily McConnell

1924: Miss R Robb

1926: Brother McIntyre (Member of the Apprentice Boys of Derry Parent Club)

1927: Brother M S Moore HML (Member of the No Surrender Parent Club)

1928: Brother Robinson (Member of the No Surrender Parent Club)

1929: Master Samuel Craig and Master Samuel Donaghy

1930: Brother John Ferguson (Past-President of the Browning Parent Club)

1931: Brother William Downes (He was initiated into the old Campise Club. The Browning Club was later formed from members of the Campise Club and Old Williamite Club)

1932: Masters W Mowbray and Robert Goodman (son of brother S Mowbray President of the Murray Parent Club)

1933: Brother William Downes (Member of the Browning Parent Club)

1934: Brother Alex McIntyre (Member of the Apprentice Boys of Derry Parent Club)

1935: Brother William Young (President of the Mitchelburne Parent Club)

1936: Lady Craigavon

1937: Master Billy White (7 years old, son of Brother James White Secretary of the Belfast Branch of the Browning Club)

1938: Master Bobby Finlay (son of Councillor R J Finlay of the Baker Club)

1939: Mrs D Norrie

1940: Brother William Ewart (Banbridge Branch of the Apprentice Boys of Derry Club)

1941: Master Samuel Warke (son of the Walker Club President)

1942: Brother Joseph Mitchell (President of the Mitchelburne Parent Club)

1943: Brother Robert Wright (14 years old and the youngest Member of the No Surrender Parent Club)

1944: Brother Emerson (Oldest Member of the Belfast Branch of the Browning Club)

1945: Brother John McCall, JP (President of the Holywood Branch Baker Club)

1946: Brother John Harte (President of the Murray Parent Club)

1947: Brother A McNeice (President of the Ballymena Branch of the Apprentice Boys Club)

1948: Brother William Johnston (Member of the Apprentice Boys of Derry Parent Club for 47 years)

1949: Brother Daniel Thompson (Member of the Mitchelburne Parent Club for over 50 years)

1950: Brother W Craig (Lieutenant Governor of the Apprentice Boys of Derry)

1951: Brother C D Milligan (President of the Browning Parent Club and Association historian)

1952: Master Raymond Lapsley (7 year old son of General Treasurer of the Apprentice Boys of Derry)

1953: Mrs Rebecca Jackson (87 years old and mother of Bobby Jackson Senior – Lundy Builder and the oldest Orange Woman in Londonderry)

1954: Brother Campbell and grandson Master John Canning (6 years old)

1955: Brother James Leslie (25 years Chaplain to the Apprentice Boys of Derry Parent Club)

1956: Brother Marshall McKay (Dungannon, Secretary of the Walker Club)

1957: Brother Alexander Thompson (President of the Mitchelburne Parent Club)

1958: Brother William Mackey (Ballyarnett, Member of the No Surrender Club for over 50 years)

1959: Mrs Rebecca Jackson (93 years old)

1960: Brother John McCullough (Ballymena, Secretary of the Baker Branch Club)

1961: Mrs Miller (Widow of David Wilson, Founder Member of the Campise Parent Club)

1962: Brother R J Smyth JP (Belfast Branch of the Murray Club and Chairman of the Belfast and District Amalgamated Committee of the Apprentice Boys for over 20 years)

1963: Brother W J Henderson JP (Belfast Total Abstinence Branch of the Apprentice Boys of Derry Club)

1964: Brother Samuel Plews (86 years old, Member of the Walker Parent Club)

1965: Brother Albert McCartney (Councillor, Hon Secretary of Mitchelburne Parent Club)

1966: Brother R Simpson (82 years old, No Surrender Parent Club)

1967: Mrs R Jackson (wife of Bobby Senior, the Lundy Builder)

1968: Brother Charles McDowell (Belfast, Past Chairman of the Belfast Amalgamated Clubs of the Apprentice Boys and last person to light Lundy on Walker's Pillar)

1969: Brother Bobby Jackson (Burning of Lundy was banned this year)

1970: Brother Bobby Jackson (Society Street Car Park)

1971: Brother Peden McKee (Secretary of the Campsie Parent Club)

1972: Brother Lynn (Murray Club)

1973: Brother Thomas Diver (Secretary of the Apprentice Boys of Derry Parent Club)

1974: Brother Thomas McClay (Walker Parent Club)

1975: Brother Samuel Foster (President of the Mitchelburne Parent Club)

1976: Master Alastair Davis (6 years old, grandson of Samuel Craig, Governor of the Apprentice Boys of Derry)

1977: Brother Maurice Adair (President of the Browning Parent Club)

1978: Brother Raymond Walker (President of the Baker Parent Club)

1979: Brother Frank Orr (61 years old and youngest Member of the Campsie Parent Club)

1980: Brother James McCelland and Grandson James (Murray Parent Club)

1981: Mrs Averil Kitson (Wife of the President of the Apprentice Boys of Derry Club)

1982: Brother William Grey (Scotland, Irvine Branch of the Walker Club)

1983: Brother Andrew McCartney (President of the Mitchelburne Parent Club)

1984: Brother William McFaul (President of the No Surrender Parent Club)

1985: Brother Albert Jackson (Chaplain, Walker Parent Club and Lundy builder)

A List of those who placed a wreath on the Apprentice Boys of Derry Mound in the churchyard of St Columb's Cathedral, on Lundy's Day.

1971: Brother Norman Millar (President of the Campise Parent Club and the first to place a wreath on the Apprentice Boys Mound)
1972: Brother Thomas Lynn (Chaplain, Murray Parent Club)
1973: Brother Stewart Heatley (Past-President of Apprentice Boys of Derry Parent Club)
1974: Brother R J Ferris (President of the Walker Parent Club)
1975: Brother Samuel Foster (President of the Mitchelburne Parent Club)
1976: Brother Albert Kilpatrick (President of the No Surrender Parent Club)
1977: Brother Maurice Adair (President of the Browning Parent Club)
1978: Brother Raymond Walker (President of the Baker Parent Club)
1979: Brother William Moore (President of the Campise Parent Club)
1980: Brother James Gordon (President of the Murray Parent Club)
1981: Brother Victor Kitson (President of the Apprentice Boys of Derry Club)
1982: Brother Samuel Heatley (Governor of the Apprentice Boys of Derry)
1983: Brother Robert Moody (Vice-President of the Mitchelburne Parent Club)

1984: Brother William McFaul (President of the No Surrender Parent Club)
1985: President of the Walker Parent Club

Bibliography

Alexander, Eleanor. *Primate Alexander Archbishop of Armagh* (London, 1913)

Colby, Thomas. *Colby's Ordnance Survey Memoir of Londonderry* (Dublin, 1837)

Childe-Pemberton, William S. *The Earl Bishop* Vols 1&2 (London, 1924)

Farrell, Sean. *Rituals and Riots* (Kentucky, 2000)

Fraser, T G. *The Irish Parading Tradition* (London, 2000)

Graham, John. *Derriana, consisting of a History of the Siege of Londonderry and Defence of Enniskillen in 1688 and 1689.* (Londonderry, 1823. Toronto, 1851)

Hempton, John. *The Siege and History of Londonderry* (Londonderry, 1861)

Kelly, William. *The Sieges of Derry* (Dublin, 2001)

Lacy, Brian. *Siege City* (Belfast, 1990)

Miller, Derek. *Still Under Siege* (Lurgan, 1989)

Milligan, C D. *Browning Memorials* (Londonderry, 1952)

Milligan, C D. *Colonel John Mitchelburne, The Centenary of the Revival of the Mitchelburne Club* (Londonderry, 1954)

Milligan, C D. *The Murray Club Centenary* (Londonderry, 1947)

Milligan, C D. *The Walker Club Centenary* (Londonderry, 1944)

Milligan, C D. *The Walls of Derry* (Londonderry, Part 1 1948 & Part 2 1950)

Mitchell, Gardiner S. *Three Cheers for the Derry's* (Londonderry, 2008)

Mullin, T H. *Derry Londonderry* (Coleraine, 1986)

McBride, Ian. *The siege of Derry in Ulster Protestant Mythology* (Dublin, 1997)

McClelland, Aiken. *William Johnston of Ballykilbeg* (Lurgan. 1990)

Simpson, Robert. *The Annals of Derry* (Londonderry, 1847)

Other Publications

Apprentice Boys of Derry Parent Club Bicentenary 1814-2014

Browning Club Centenary of its revival 1861-1961

The 300th Anniversary of the Association of the Apprentice Boys of Derry 1714-2014

Official Brochure of the Tercentenary Celebrations of the Apprentice Boys of Derry Association

Disturbances In Northern Ireland (Belfast, 1969)

Newspapers

The Londonderry Sentinel.
The Londonderry Journal.
The Londonderry Guardian.
Londonderry Standard.
Belfast Telegraph.
Belfast Newsletter.

BIBLIOGRAPHY

Unpublished Sources

Jackson family private archives.
Details of the Lundy builders from the 1930s onward were personally described by the late Robert Jackson Junior, who read the Lundy Builders manuscript and added further details about the various characters mentioned within it before his death. Corrections were also made to ensure its accuracy.

Oil Paintings

An unfinished oil painting by Mr Robert Jackson (1927-2016) of Lundy hanging from Walker's Pillar is currently on display in the Apprentice Boys of Derry Museum. It was painted around the early eighties.

In the Derry City Museum, oil painting of the burning of Lundy, artist unknown, 1830.

Lundy Effigy – Tower Museum (Union Hall place Londonderry)

There is an eighteen-foot effigy of Colonel Robert Lundy gifted by Mr Robert Jackson to the Tower Museum in perpetuity. This particular effigy was displayed in Kennedy Street as part of the Tercentenary Siege of Londonderry, August Celebrations. The uniform worn is identical to the final Lundy effigy, made by the Jackson family on behalf of the Apprentice Boys of Derry Association. Due to height restriction in the museum, only the upper torso is displayed along with other items of uniform. Mr Robert Jackson gifted it to the Tower Museum in 1990.

APPENDIX 1

Bishop of Derry Frederick Hervey, 4th Earl of Bristol (better known as Mitred Fred), became Bishop of Derry in 1768. He rapidly established himself as a champion of the people in the Anglo-Irish political arena. Hervey supported Catholic Emancipation, opposed the Penal Laws and was refreshingly free from all religious bigotry, being an Englishman. This was a step forward for the dissenting churches in the City and beyond. In 1784 Father John Lynch began to construct the Long Tower Church and Bishop Hervey gave £200 towards the building cost, as well as to the building of Presbyterian churches both in and beyond the City. Hervey was not always as generous in his giving to the latter. Bishop Hervey deemed Presbyterians *"much more dangerous than the Papists"*[19] for their principles were truly republican. Hervey believed that an over indulgence to the Presbyterians and the Papists could actually save the Kingdom from falling into the same state as the American colonies.

Bishop Hervey was closely involved with the Volunteers, who were raised to defend Ireland against the French. However, the militia quickly became affected by events in America and in Ireland, and thus developed into a potentially menacing force. Hervey himself was Colonel of the Londonderry Corps of Volunteers in 1783 and his forthright opinions

---

19 Curle, John. *The Honourable the Irish Society*. (2004) p 216

put him in a bad light with some elements within the Protestant ascendancy. The Bishop was under the impression that if he could win the overall leadership of the Volunteers, he could then use his position within the movement as a means to forward his reforms, i.e. Irish legislative and judicial independence, along with the relaxation of the penal laws and general liberalisation. To some extent the Bishop was successful; he received a donation from the Irish Society to the Volunteers in 1781 to help further his cause. The British Government, however, saw Volunteers as a dangerous organisation and for some time had the Bishop shadowed by spies. At the Volunteer Convention in Dublin in 1783, the Episcopal Volunteer Bishop's ideologies were defeated by Lord Charlemont's more moderate supporters and the Bishop returned to Londonderry embittered by what had taken place. He never again got deeply involved in the politics of his adopted land. In December 1791, the Earl Bishop left Ireland never to return. He used his bad health as an excuse, but in reality he had tried to force political issues in Ireland too far too soon and Ireland was neither ready nor prepared to make such changes. Equally his connections in France, Rome, England and with the Volunteer movement in Ireland made him a dangerous man. The British Government feared that through his leadership a revolt could occur in Ireland, spilling over onto the mainland.

The very term "Lundy," according to the Dictionary of Slang states that a Lundy is a collaborator, a traitor who is suspected of Catholic sympathies by the Protestant community. The Bishop's political views, reform bills and his military position placed him in juxtaposition with another Colonel, who was also in Command of militia within the City. He was seen as a champion of the people, but would later emerge as a traitor to the Protestant cause in Londonderry, namely Robert Lundy.

Horace Walpole in 1783 declared that the *"Bristol-Derry by his popish sympathies was qualifying for a Cardinal's hat; others accused him of hostility to the Government."*[20]

---

20   Childe-Pemberton, William S. *The Earl Bishop.* (1924) Vol 1 p 300

www.ingramcontent.com/pod-product-compliance
Lightning Source LLC
Chambersburg PA
CBHW072051110526
44590CB00018B/3126